ŚŪDRAS IN MANU

ŚŪDRAS IN MANU

CHITRA TIWARI

With a Foreword by
SRI JAGJIWAN RAM

MOTILAL BANARSIDASS PUBLISHERS
PRIVATE LIMITED • DELHI

Reprint : Delhi, 2017
First Edition : Delhi, 1963

ISBN: 978-81-208-4101-7 (Cloth)
ISBN: 978-81-208-4117-8 (Paper)

Also available at
MOTILAL BANARSIDASS
41 U.A., Bungalow Road, Jawahar Nagar, Delhi 110 007
8 Mahalaxmi Chamber, 22 Bhulabhai Desai Road, Mumbai 400 026
203 Royapettah High Road, Mylapore, Chennai 600 004
236, 9th Main III Block, Jayanagar, Bengaluru 560 011
8 Camac Street, Kolkata 700 017
Ashok Rajpath, Patna 800 004
Chowk, Varanasi 221 001

MLBD Cataloging-in-Publication Data
ŚŪDRAS IN MANU
by CHITRA TIWARI
with a Foreword by JAGJIWAN RAM
ISBN: 978-81-208-4101-7 (HB)
ISBN: 978-81-208-4117-8 (PB)
Includes Index
I. Hinduism II. Status of Śūdras III. Manu Smriti
IV. Tiwari, Chitra V. Ram, Jagjiwan

Printed in India
by RP Jain at NAB Printing Unit,
A-44, Naraina Industrial Area, Phase I, New Delhi–110028
and published by JP Jain for Motilal Banarsidass Publishers (P) Ltd.,
41 U.A. Bungalow Road, Jawahar Nagar, Delhi-110007

TO THE DEAD PAST AND
THE GLORIOUS FUTURE
OF THE ŚŪDRAS

CONTENTS

PREFACE

This little piece of research had been guided by the late Dr. R. S. Tripathi, M.A., Ph.D. (London), Professor and Head of the Department of History, Benares Hindu University, about a decade ago, when I was a student. It is unfortunate that he is no more and cannot see this work in print. I remember him with the deepest gratitude.

I am indebted to Sri Jagjivan Ram for very kindly finding time from his preoccupying cabinet engagements to write an encouraging Foreword to this book. It has added greatly to the worth of the work. My thanks are due also to Messrs Motilal Banarsidass, the distinguished publishers of oriental works, for making this book available to the reading public, and to Sri Markandeya Upadhyaya, M. A., for doing the Index.

I trust this little venture will find favour with my readers and will prove helpful to those working to better the lot of our condemned toilers, the Śūdras. The past has been too long with us and the memory attaching to the destiny of this unfortunate mass of humanity too severe. And yet, the intransigence of the privileged castemen notwithstanding, the dawn of integration is not far to break over the demoniac dark of distinction.

CHITRA TIWARI

Calcutta,
8. 10. 1963

FOREWORD

I readily accepted to write a Foreword to this precious little document. But due to my preoccupation with more urgent work, I could not go through the manuscript for an abnormally long time and hence this Foreword was much delayed. This piece of research is written by a young student, Miss Chitra Upadhyaya. The work deals dipassionately with the origin, types, duties, occupations, status—social, economic and legal—of the Sudras, the Mixed Castes and the Untouchables as reflected in the Code of Manu. All relevant literature seems to have been studied and data relating to the subject collected. The Bibliography appended to the composition indicates the range and scope of such study. The material has been treated with great thoroughness and the conclusions are fair. The ease and felicity with which the author handles her data would indeed do credit to a scholar of repute. The work is fully documented and its method bears the stamp of scientific scholarship.

The subject chosen for study is very proper as the origin of the Bahiṣkrit Śūdras or the excluded castes is yet to be authoritatively determined. But it incidently reflects the spirit of the times as also the zeal which is agitating our younger minds to undo the wrong done to countless numbers of Indian humanity degrading these multitudinous masses to a state of abject triviality. And it is in the fitness of things that those same should have found a champion of their cause in the daughter of a community which in many quarters is supposed to have accomplished the wrong. The boldness with which the young scholar has attacked social inequity at places in course of her investigation thus stands justified.

I am further gratified to learn that Miss Upadhyaya is the grand-daughter of that brilliant son of Bihar, the late Shri Harnandan Pandey of the Archaeological Survey of India, whom the cruel hand of death removed from our midst in full youth. I hope this dissertation, full of verve, when put in print, will find favour with the reading public and while commending it, I dare say, it will repay reading.

4th February, 1954 — Jagjiwan Ram

NEW DELHI

CHAPTER I

INTRODUCTORY

The scope and extent of this dissertation is limited to the Code of Manu. Śūdras and their numerous sub-castes, besides the much maligned untouchables, have found mention in some form or other in various law-texts both before and after Manu. The problems relating to them, despite a few commendable attempts, are still a desideratum.

References to Śūdras and allied castes in other ancient documents are succinct and hazy and they do not tell us in any detail about the status, the duties and the rights of those castes, and consequently no clear and conclusive estimate of their social life can be formed. Manu is clear and unambiguous in his expression and although extremely summary, partial and even dogmatic in his treatment of them, the great law-giver presents a detailed code and marshals their duties and penalties in unequivocal terms. His *Smṛti* therefore is the best we have on record in way of ancient legislation on the subject.

His *Smṛti* therefore we shall make our main authority, not forgetting that despite the *Manusmṛti*'s bold and exhaustive treatment the source is, nevertheless, to be supplemented here and there by unimpeachable documents and texts. But certainly they will only be treated as auxiliaries adding to, delimiting or elucidating the context and the purport of Manu. No code in ancient times commanded such esteem as did the Code of Manu and none was fuller or even as full as this remarkable piece of legislation despite its inequitous, even partial and cruel character in certain circumstances and details.

It will not be out of place here to mention that prior to Manu history had known only two codes—those of Hammurabi and Moses coming respectively from about the twentieth and the Sixteenth centuries B.C. Of these the latter is nothing but a series of domestic commandments and the former, howsoever detailed and extraordinary, is a brief document containing royal commands on various topics of state administration and property rights. Manu's Code on the contrary towers high over all such documents of antiquity, for in a consummate treatise it orders the life of the individual from long before he is born to long after he is dead. So also does it plan out the activities of a settled and ordered humanity in all its social patterns. It registers and recounts all that had come down to its days in way of social habits, customs and usages, positive pieces of legislation as reflected in earlier works, and it even endorses, declaims and recreates, where need be, types of social behaviour considered fit by the eminent law-giver. Being one of the most ancient codes of the Hindu society, it has rightly commanded enormous respect and its authority has seldom been questioned.

This is mainly the reason why much of what may be considered inequitious, partial or even derogatory to the status of certain sections of the community, its authority has remained unassailable through centuries. And this is the reason why we also are making this great document the subject of our present study.

Numerous commentaries and glosses have been written to elucidate the meaning and purport of the passages of the *Manusmṛti* and it will be our endeavour to find and cite all such references that bear upon our subject relevently so that the social condition under our review may receive the necessary light. Our main work of reliance, however, besides the original text of Manu, will be the renowned commentary of Kullūkabhaṭṭa entitled the *Manwarthamuktāvalīsaṁvalitā*.

A number of modern works are devoted to the study of social life and allied subjects, such as *The Origin of Caste* by Senart, *The History of Caste in India* by Ketkar, *Life in Ancient India in the Age of the Mantras* by Aiyangar, *Social and Religious Life in Gṛhyasūtras* by Apte, *Some Aspects of the Earliest Social History of India* by Sarkar, *Social Life in Ancient India* by Chakladar, and numerous others. But while they treat of Hindu social polity as a whole they hardly touch upon the Śūdra problem: a discussion regarding the origin of Śūdras, their consequent deterioration as also an investigation into the expansion and the legal, economic, political and social status of Antyajas,

Aspṛśyas and like others have escaped their notice. As a matter of fact, a fuller treatment of the subject is now imperative as the march of time has brought the Śūdra and the likes of him to the level of other higher castes of the Hindu community in at least the legal and political spheres. the present setting of things does not only question the propriety of ancient caste distinctions but, in addition, discountenances them most positively thus levelling down all legal and political privileges to an even ground. There is therefore no wonder why even such a sacrosanct authority as Manu will not hold. It is therefore again that scholars like Ambedkar have come out with bold denunciations of the Dharmaśāstras in support of the rights of the Śūdras and the Untouchables. We have carefully considered the facts collected by the eminent legislator in his books bearing on the Śūdras and Untouchables but we are afraid that, despite the vigour with which the subject has been treated in those admirable volumes, Dr. Ambedkar's stand has unfortunately been rendered partisan. His conclusions therefore have been coloured with deep-seated prejudices and his findings have taken the form of a relentless attack unrelieved by suggestive approach or academic investigation. His conclusions in a number of cases are acceptable but many besides them are vitiated by a frontal attack and are so rendered, at least partially, ineffective.

Another admirable study of the Śūdras has been attempted in recent years by Bhupendra Nath Datta in his *Studies in Indian Social Polity*. But although Śūdras have found a searching treatment there the discussion regarding them carried on from an ethnological point of view covers a long range, and yet being a mere part of the whole, is ultimately lost in the surrounding bulk of figures and facts. While the debt to Bhupendra Nath Datta of scholars of social polity investigating mainly into the ethnic field is considerable, a readable account of the Śūdras, and the Untouchables and of their environments is still lacking.

Hence it calls for a clear marshalling of data on the background of a short canvas reflecting them back in broad contours. The *Manusmṛti* provides that canvas. Manu for the first time, and for that matter also perhaps for the last, has treated exhaustively of the status, duties and punishments of the

Śūdras and has enumerated the in-betweens of the castes as also the Untouchables. Manu's range being short, the Śūdras and the Untouchables show in vivid colours and their study in their various vicissitudes will certainly be fruitful. An attempt here therefore is made to give in one place a readable account of the Śūdras and the Untouchables as gleaned from Manu.

In order that the part may not be lost in the whole light has been thrown only on the Śūdras and the Untouchables; and it is to make their position and circumstances indubitably clear that comparison at times has been drawn between their privileges and penalties and those of the upper castes. The discussion is naturally and to the best possibilities academic and to that extent, it hardly need mention, the present dissertation adds to the existing knowledge of things regarding the Śūdras and the Untouchables.

Following a wave of revivalism there has been in recent years a tendency to justify the castes. They cannot be defended on any ground, social, moral or ethical. The Hindu community has suffered beyond reparation through long corridors of time from the caste system which has segregated as unclean and pariah vast multitudes of Indian humanity who not only have not had any rights under the sun but have had to live out of the town and the village, indeed beyond the pale of civilization. It is heartening that the hold of this octopus, however slowly, is, after all, loosening on the community and the day may not be far when man will take his due place in the order of things.

The following chapters of this thesis will academically investigate into (1) the variety of the Śūdras and other Lower Castes and their sub-castes and divisions, their progressive formation and additions, (2) their social status, marriage, duties and rights, inheritance, etc., (3) their religious status, (4) legal and political status, and (5) their economic condition. Thus for the first time and in one place an attempt will be made to study the Śūdras and allied castes as envisaged in the *Manusmṛti*.

This dissertation poses new problems and in certain incidents challenges old views, like *Varṇa* considered as colour of the skin or Śūdras made to represent a stock distinct from the Aryan; and even if the conclusions may not be final they will at least register new view-points and provoke fresh investigation.

Relevant literature, both text and derivative, has been carefully studied in this regard and references, where necessary, have been cited to elucidate the findings and support the conclusions. A list of works bearing on the subject and alluded to in course of this dissertation is appended to this study.

The *Manusmṛti* itself undoubtedly is a Brahman document probably written during the epoch of Brahman revivalism led by Puṣyamitra Śuṅga, the General and Purohita of Bṛhadratha, the last of the line of the illustrious Mauryas whom the Brahman usurper killed thus supplanting the rule of the Mauryas. The present redaction was perhaps finalised during the rule of the Imperial Guptas but the kernel as also its main principles and various details were composed without doubt during the Śuṅga epoch of the second century B. C. The Code, although it reflects its times, has, nevertheless, remained throughout the later centuries down to the present day the main authority on social and legal matters and thus it may naturally reflect equally the social trends of later times.

CHAPTER II

THE ORIGIN OF THE ŚŪDRAS

Before we undertake to enumerate the various sections and sub-sections of Śūdras and the Untouchables as laid down in the Code of Manu it will be imperative to investigate into the ethnic environs of these castes. But even before treating that aspect of our study it will be natural to enquire as to how and when they arose or found a place in the complicated caste system. As a matter of fact, a passing glance at the caste system itself in that case will become important and the antecedents of the Śūdra before he comes to be treated in the pages of Manu a fruitful object of enquiry which will help the understanding of his status in the celebrated Code.

We know that despite the existence in many lands and communities of stereotyped social sections and sub-sections, the caste system, as we know it to-day, is peculiar to India. To be Hindu is not quite enough for one has to belong not only to one of its major divisions but further to a sub-caste, even to a section or sub-section of such a sub-caste and to conform to its rigid and peculiar usages and angularities. This is why conversion has no place in Hinduism, and although not positively always forbidden by mandatory injunctions, it has been rendered totally ineffective by attending circumstances, for, as pointed out above, Hinduism is not one vast sheet of humanity like Christianity or Islam where it is enough mere to enter in order to get absorbed; one has to belong to a particular section whose customs and usages, rights and duties are not conferred by the mere choice of the convert-initiate but have to be inherited, and where, in effect, birth becomes the deciding factor. This is why when in recent years conversion on a large scale was attempted and in great numbers people of other persuations entered the fold of Hinduism no place could be found for them and, facing great trouble in the sphere of interdining and intermarriage, they had to go back from where they had come.

The caste system is a huge complex composed of various factors. Races and invasions, codes and institutions of distinct epochs of Indian history have left their indelible marks on the society. The, entire complex has got to be analysed and its characteristics and components explained. Sociologists assert and correctly that when a class becomes incrusted by denying connubium and commensality with other classes, the class turns itself into a caste. Indian castes are naturally exclusive groups, practising endogamy and interdicting interdining with persons of other castes. One has to marry within a sub-caste and beyond the forbidden degrees while the dining is restricted to special subsectional extents. Each caste and sub-caste has got its own rules and regulations for the preservation of its integrity. This is the present state of the Indian caste system where the Śūdras and the Untouchables have their inevitable place and all this has been the subject of unlimited elaboration in the pages of Manu. But the question is, Has it always been so ? In other words, What are the antecedents and authorities of Manu ?

The first reference to the caste system and to the Śūdra occurs in a late hymn of the *Ṛgveda* in its famous Puruṣasūkta (X 90, 12) :

ब्राह्मणोऽस्य मुखमासीद् बाहू राजन्यः कृतः ।
ऊरू तदस्य यद्वैश्यः पद्भ्यां शूद्रोऽअजायत ॥

"The Brāhmaṇa sprang from the mouth, the Kṣatriya from the arms, the Vaiśya from the thighs and the Śūdra from the feet (of the Creator)".

This passage of the *Ṛgveda* has been declared a fabrication and an interpolation, which may or may not have been the case, although the fact remains that the context is located in a late section of the great document. This circumstance, however, does not discredit the view that after all the text is vedic and has at any rate been repeated in the *Vājasaneya Saṁhitā* of the *Yajurveda* (31, 11) which settles its venerable ancient character. The ancestral lives of the great sages and of those of their royal benefactors prove the existence of the Brahman and the Kshatriya castes in the *Ṛgveda* from its earliest strata; and the reference to the *Viś*, the vast multitude of commoners, presents a plea for the existence of the Vaiśyas too during the Rigvedic times. The existence of Śūdras during vedic times has been certainly doubted, even challenged, by some although their vedic origin can hardly be assailed. The passage of the *Ṛgveda* may be late but is at least coeval in time with that referred to above of the white *Yajurveda*. Indeed, occurring as it does among the hymns borrowed from the *Ṛgveda*, it may with considerable strength be even asserted that the fact of the Śūdra being Rigvedic can hardly be doubted although it is certain that we do not find a trace of untouchability in the sacred records of the vedic texts in the form and to the extent it obtains in India to-day. Senart correctly thinks that in fact the caste system in the form of social groupings had its inception in the united Aryo-Iranian period of the history of Indo-Europeans because the names of three Persian upper classes agree with those of the Indian ones. Only the Śūdra is absent there and he may have thus been a social entity of the Indian castes. The question which now we have to answer is—Do the Śūdras represent a distinct ethnic unit or are they drawn from an extraction independent of the vedic Aryan race ?

This readily brings us to an allied important enquiry, that of the *Varṇa*. Scholars invariably seek to derive the castes from *varṇa* "colour". There is no doubt about the fact that almost throughout the Indian tradition and literature the castes have been referred to by the single term *Varṇa*, and Manu himself throughout his Code alludes to the castes through his terms *Sarvavarṇa*, *Varṇa*, *Caturvarṇa* and the like. But whether the term *Varṇa* technically ever indicated the varying shades of colour of the people who were ultimately indicated through those shades is doubtful. We are not unaware of the implication of colour, howsoever distant, implied by the term *varṇa* but whether that implication has remained the guiding principle and the ruling factor of the term through the centuries during which it has been used is yet a desideratum. It may be argued that the implication has been so patent that the contrary has never been sought to be established nor the basic purport ever questioned; but it can be likewise answered that many a time the misuse rather than the use of the implied purport of a term conditions its usage.

The word *varṇa* does indicate colour or light in several

passages of the *Ṛgveda*.[1] In a general sense also sometimes groups of people have been alluded as having dark or fair colour. The *Taittirīya Brāhmaṇa* refers to Brahmans of divine varṇa and to Śūdra as of the *asūryamvarṇa*.[2] Here it can be clearly seen that status more than colour is the distinction sought to be covered by the word *varṇa*. Kane, however, in his *History of Dharmaśāstra*[3] seeks to use the reference of the *Tai. Br.* for explaining the Rigvedic verse IX. 71,2 and its phrase *asūryamvarṇa* to mean the Śūdṛa tribe which, however, cannot be accepted.

The western indologists distinguish the Śūdras from the Aryans as the original inhabitants of India, a dark-skinned people conquered and subjugated by their white-skinned Aryan masters. This view they seek to corroborate by identifying the Śūdras with the dark-coloured Dāsas and Dasyus who find mention in numerous passages of the *Ṛgveda*.[4] There is no doubt about the fact that the Dāsas and Dasyus are identical and sometimes they occur in the same verses referring to the same enemy.[5] But seldom have the Śūdras been identified with either the Dāsas or Dasyus except perhaps where an opprobrious epithet is meant. The various epithets characterizing the look, language, and belief of the Dāsas and Dasyus—e.g. *anāsāḥ* (snubnosed), *mṛdhravācaḥ* (of harsh and indistinct speech), *avrata* (not conforming to the Aryan ceremonies), *akratu* (not performing sacrifices), *Śiśnadevāḥ* (phallic worshippers). And certainly nowhere have the vedic gods been sought to hurl their deadly weapons on the Śūdras or to protect the Aryan from them as in case with the Dāsas and Dasyus.

Indeed it will be dangerous to build the interpretation regarding castes on the basis of colour—*white* (*śubhra* or Ārya), the copper (*tāmra*), and the black *kṛṣṇa*)—as instances are not wanting where traditionally even the wholly white nordic people have been divided on the basis of colour. The fundamental factor of the Aryans having been a white race itself is not entirely unvulnerable and ethnologists are not

[1] I. 73. 7; II. 3, 5; IX. 97, 15; IX. 104, 4; IX. 105, 4; X. 124. 7.

[2] I. 2. 6. [3] p. 25.

[4] I. 51. 8; I. 103, 3; I. 117, 21; II. 11, 2, 4, 18, 19; III. 29, 9; V. 70, 3; VII. 5, 6; IX. 88, 4; VI. 18, 3; VI. 25, 2.

[5] *Ṛv.* X. 22, 8, X. 99, 6.

lacking in number who have questioned the propriety and sanity of such a conclusion. But accepting with the popular belief the fact of the Indo-Aryans having been fair in complexion, we have to accept along with it, on the evidence of the vedic texts themselves, that among the Rigvedic ṛṣis there were those who were positively of a dark colour which always was not incidental to mixed breeding. The *Ṛgveda* calls Kaṇva *kṛṣṇa*, black, in colour,[1] and consequently the entire line of the Kāṇvāyanas may have been dark. Regarding ṛṣis of questionable birth and even of a dark shade of colour who had been accepted as leaders and seers among the Aryans mention may be made of Kavaṣa Ailūṣa[2], Vatsa,[3] Kakṣīvān Auśija[4] and Satyakāma Jābāla.[5] Of these Kavaṣa Ailūṣa of the *Aitareya Br.*[6] has already been mentioned in the *Ṛgveda* and is the seer of the hymn 30 of that *Veda*. Besides these vedic ṛṣis many of the Hindu heroes and heroines of the epics were dark. Again the scanty trace of any blond characteristics either in the Indian population or in the ancient literature is of debatable origin.

It is true that the Vedas speak of the *Ārya-varṇa* and *Dāsa-varṇa* and the Smṛtis of the four *varṇas* typifying the four castes, but that the word '*varṇa*' means 'skin-colour' yet remains hypothetical. For, in that case we shall have to accept another very unacceptable principle that the people of the Punjab were *during the vedic times* composed of all the four Blumenbach races—the white (Caucasian), the red (American, aboriginal), the yellow (Mongolian) and the black (Negroid). Now the question which naturally occurs to the mind is : if the white-skinned Brahman belonged to the white Indo-European race and the Śūdra to the black negroid one, to which races then did the red Kṣatriya and the yellow Vaiśya belong ? This interpretation is indeed absurd on the very face of it. Hindu scriptures offer a different and more logical explanation when they interpret the colours as typifying diverse professions. The priest or the Brahmaṇ is described *śubhra*, white, for as a religious functionary he typified purity and the emblem of purity is white. Service

[1] X. 31, 11.
[2] *Kauśitaki Br.*, 12, 3.
[3] *Pañcaviṃśa Br.*, 14, 66.
[4] *Ṛv.*, I. 18, 1.
[5] *Chāndogya Upa.*, VI. 4, 4.
[6] 8, 1.

is soiled, hence the servile Śūdra is black. Hence social stratification based on difference of skin-colour is not only untenable but has to be dismissed as a pan-Germanic myth.

The profession itself in vedic times was not completely and strictly a matter of non-transgression. At least the Brahman could choose vocations that suited his temper. The Rigvedic sage sings : "Myself am a bard, my father is a physician, my mother a stone-grinder. Thus planning in various wages, desirous of wealth, we live following (others) like cattle, flow Soma, flow for Indra's sake".[1] In this case if acquisition of wealth could be planned so as to include even the so-called derogatory avocations, where did the stigma attach ? The profession of the physician and meanial work like stone-grinding which have through centuries been considered low in India could not transfer the parents of the Rigvedic bard to the lowly state of the Śūdra and even if it were to effect this, certainly the stock of the Aryan bard could never have changed to that of the aboriginal Dāsas and Dasyus.

After showing that the Śūdras cannot be transferred to the aboriginal Dāsa and Dasyu stock on the vulnerable interpretation of *varṇa*, we can now be positive in asserting that they originally beloged to the Āryan group. The most important evidence in this regard is the *Puruṣasūkta* itself where the entire Aryan body-politic is sought to be divided among vocational groups. We must not forget in this connection that it is one body—the body of Prajāpati—which is sacrificed and that it is parts of the self-same body which furnish the four strata of the Aryan society. Therefore any attempt to transfer the root and origin of any of the constituents of the body of the Creator—Brāhmaṇa representing the mouth, Kṣatriya representing the arms, Vaiśya representing the thighs and Śūdra representing the feet—would be non-vedic and would militate against the most sacred and unimpeachable authority, the *Ṛgveda*, which is the only contemporary document standing at the head of our sources of information on the point.

Nor is the tradition or chain of this evidence lacking in later literature. Both the *Bhagavadgītā* and our field of investigation the *Manusmṛti* trail and confirm the tradition.

[1] *Ṛv.*, IX. 112, 3.

The former of these make Kṛṣṇa (God) create the four *varṇas* according to their nature (*guṇa*) and actions (*karma*, work). The text reads : *cāturvarṇyam mayā sṛṣṭam guṇakarma-vibhāgaśaḥ.*[1] Here again all the four castes are accepted as of one stock and as God Himself (like Prajāpati of the Rigvedic *Puruṣasūkta*) creating them and ordering the respective spheres of their activities. Here we must remember that while the divisions are made in consequence of the work of the *varṇas* all the four are simultaneously created out of a common original whole to which the Śūdra is as much a part as is the Brahman.

Manu likewise asserts that there are Four and Four *Varṇas* alone and never a Fifth— *nāsti tu pañcamaḥ*[2]—and he reckons Śūdra as the Fourth. This clearly distinguishes the character of Śūdras from that of the numerous other hybrid (*saṅkara*) inter castes and the Untouchables and unfailingly points their place among the Varṇas. Indeed the very next[3] verse of the *Manusmṛti* while describing the scope of its discussions broadly divides the humanity whose duties it essays to ordain into two broad divisions, those of the *Varṇas* and those again of the *Antarprabhavas* (i.e. of the original Four Varṇas—Brāhmaṇa, Kṣatriya, Vaiśya and Śūdra—and of the mixed castes which arose from the union of sexes between dissimilar castes. This clearly indicates that Manu, like the *Ṛgveda* and the *Bhagavadgītā*, places the Śūdras along with the Dvijas in the same stock and clearly distinguishes them from the Untouchables who may or may not have belonged to the original extraction of the Four Varṇas. There is evidence to show that some at least among the Untouchables too came from the original Aryan stock. But of that in due context.

To this positive record we must add that negative evidence which we have quoted elsewhere above that the Śūdra could not have belonged to the stock of the Dāsas and Dasyus as the epithets used for the latter could never apply to the Śūdras. Thus the cumulative evidence of the most sacred documents —the *Ṛgveda*, the *Bhagavadgītā* and the *Manusmṛti*—trebly

[1] VIII. 13.
[2] X. 4.
[3] I. 2. Also cf. ibid., I. 31.

asserts the racial homogeneity of the Śūdras with Dvijas and rules out the possibility of their having originated from the aboriginal stock.

Here we may add that the attempts of scholars like Risley[1] to establish racial types among the castes of India through measurement of head and nose have almost totally failed in their objective, for the results have shown that more often than not the Śūdra and the pariah have offered better physical features than the Brahman or the Kshatriya to the claims of being recognized as representatives of the so-called Indo-European stock. At least that would prove the contrary and would establish the stock-oneness of the Śūdras with the Dvijas. That ethnological approach, if nothing else, has at least established the fact that there is no racial basis for the difference among castes. In consequence the only irresistible alternative is the hypothesis that a caste is socio-economic grouping, and the status of a caste is determined not by the amount of leptorrhiney representing the supposed Aryan blood present in it, but by the force of class character. To this class character we shall have occasion to return again.

Again, who were the Śūdras ? Manu of course, as pointed out above, accepts them as of the original stock of which the Dvijas formed part, although he refers to another class of Śūdras that he formed for want of the performance of vedic rites. Among those who due to this reason were degraded from the status of the Kshatriya caste to the lowly position of the Śūdras he enumerates the Pauṇḍrakas, the Oḍras, Draviḍas, Kambojas, Yavanas, Śakas, Daradas, Pahlavas, Cinas, Kirātas, and Khasas.[2] Here, however, we shall have no trouble in distinguishing that the declamation of Manu has only a moral tone, for due to the non-observance of rites he condemns distinct ethnic units independent of the Aryan stock to the position of the Śūdras. On another occasion his code condemns the Śakas and Yavanas also to the Śūdra status[3] forbidding interdining between them and the twice-born. Here it need not be discussed whether the Śakas and Yavanas were originally Aryans of the Cossack

[1] Datta : *Studies in Ind. So. Polity*, pp. 104-120.

[2] *Manusmṛti*, X. 43-45.

[3] X. 44.

or the Ionian Greek type or non-Aryans. It is enough to accept with Manu that by his time, and for that matter from much earlier ages,[1] the Śakas had come to be characterized as *Mlecchas* and *Śūdras*. Manu at one place distinguishes between a free-Śūdra and a slave-Śūdra who could be bought and sold.[2] The common factor in both the cases, however, Manu maintains, is service from which the Śūdra can never gain freedom for it is for "serving the Brāhmaṇa that he was created by Svayambhū (Brahmā)."[3] Indeed Manu asserts that even if his master frees him from slavery the Śūdra has to remain servile and to perform the duties (i.e. service) of a Śūdra, for that is his natural duty.[4] Manu brands all others that are outside the range of the four varṇas as Dasyus; whether they speak the language of the Mlecchas or of Aryas, it does not matter.

Śūdra has been defined to mean one who grieves; he is called the 'child of misery'. He is called the child of *tapas* (sorrow). Bādarāyaṇa attempts an ingenious derivation of the word by quoting a story.

King Janaśruti when exclaimed at first as a Śūdra was refused the initiation into *brahmavidyā* by the Brahmans. Then he grieved and from his grief (*śocanā*) the word 'Śūdra' took its form.[5] The absurdity of this speculation warrants little comment to elucidate its emptiness. A better and more convincing derivation of the term Śūdra has been advanced by Vidhusekhar Sastri.[6] He says, "It seems to me that the word is not a pure Sanskrit one, and is derived from Sanskrit *kshudra* (small)...Now the interchange of the three sibilants,...in vedic language, even at the time of the *Saṁhitā* is found not unfrequently... Thus we have no difficulty in accounting for 'ś' in Śūdra from *kshudra*". This is apparently a fair suggestion although

[1] Cf. Patañjali's *Mahābhāṣya* on Pāṇini's शूद्राणामनिर्वसितानाम्...

[2] शूद्रं तु कारयेद्दास्यं क्रीतमक्रीतमेव वा । दास्यायैव हि सृष्टोऽसौ ब्राह्मणस्य स्वयंभुवा ॥ VIII. 413.

[3] Ibid.

[4] न स्वामिना निसृष्टोऽपि शूद्रो दास्याद्विमुच्यते ।
निसर्गजं हि तत्तस्य कस्तस्मात्तदपोहति ॥ ibid., 414.

[5] *Vedānta Sūtras*, XIII. 34.

[6] *Indian Anitquary*, Vol. Lx., 1922—Śūdra.

it might give rise to phonetical difficulties. Anyway, this catches at least on one thing, the lowly position of the people implied by the term for those who bear it.

This brings us to our suggestion that Śūdras, belonging to the original and the same stock as the twice-born, were degraded to their accepted position as a result of class-war. The expression 'class-war' makes many people prick their ears but, as a matter of fact, it should not, as every society is based on economic factors and political power gives shapes to it. Hence economic causes leading to its political expressions, politics of all times being a projection of the contemporary or anterior economics, have to be discovered in order to find out the roots of the caste-system in general and of the Śūdras in particular. As said elsewhere, when a class becomes incrusted by denying connubium and commensality with other classes, the class forms itself into a caste. The formation of caste and class may not everywhere lie in racial difference, it may be suggested with regard to the rise of castes in India, they may have evolved out of the society itself. The present day Hindu society is a congeries of endogamous and independent groups. The society is divided into vertical sections. Added to it, the present day class distinctions based no money power is playing its rôle. It is clearly the vertical sections again in horizontal lines.

After concluding that the Śūdras belonged to the same stock as the twice-born it will not be difficult to show that the same law operated in the vedic society to give rise to the Śūdras. The vast common people in the Rigvedic times were called the Viśas (*Viś*). From this vast base arose two specialized groups the priests (Brahmans) and nobles (Rājā and others—Rājanyas=Kṣatriyas), distinguished by their wealth, power and privileges from and above the common mass of people. The leftovers generally applied themselves to agriculture, cattle-breeding and such other domestic and pastoral occupations. But certainly the entire multitude of men did not follow agricultural pursuits as all the Kṣhatriyas never functioned as soldiers all the time nor did all the Brahmans ever pursue the profession of priesthood. There were those among each that sweated and toiled for living and went adding to the number of the degraded. The leftovers among the Viśas themselves might have created the big mass of the Śūdras in course of time while the latter might have worked along with the Vaiśyas and others as meanial auxiliaries as the phrase '*Śūdrāryau*' suggests (here the Ārya has the implication of the twice-born). We find from Manu himself that Vaiśya and Śūdra are almost always grouped together.[1]

But the formation of this class must have taken time. We know, as we have noted elsewhere, that the Iranian Aryans had only the three upper classes or castes and not the Śūdras and the *Ṛgveda* also mentions the Śūdra only once and that too among the last stage hymns, which shows that as agriculture expanded and wealth grew and concentrated in the hands of the three upper propertied classes (it must not be supposed that the ṛṣi-priests had no wealth of their own for the *Ṛgveda* is full of panegyrical songs and hymns lauding the munificence and benefactions of kings who showered on them, besides articles of luxury, chariots full of slaves and slave girls, cattle and gold) the ranks of the Śūdras multiplied.

Service soils the Śūdras. They are identified with the very toil.[2] The *Manusmṛti* affirms that they are created by God for serving (*dāsya*) the Brahmans.[3] Their profession sinks them low for we see that lower is the profession of a group, correspondingly lower is its social rank. Among all the upper castes perhaps there were those who took to toiling vocations; some vocations originally commendable came in course of time to be regarded low; some (Śūdras), it cannot perhaps be wholly denied, were recruited from among the enslaved conquered enemies (we have already shown that the *Manusmṛti* makes a distinction between slave and free or bought and liberated Śūdras). From a Rigvedic hymn, quoted above, itself it is evident that choice in adopting callings could be freely exercised and that while the composer of the hymn chose to remain a seer, his father had practised as a physician and his mother had applied herself to the profits of the grinding stone. "The rathakāras (chariot-makers), in early vedic times, esteemed for their skill, later became degraded because of the growth of the feeling that manual

[1] I. 116; III. 24; III. 112; VIII. 277; 418; IX. 325; X. 98; XI. 34.
[2] *S.B.E.*, Vol. 44, p. 410. Also cf. ibid., p. 446—'Śūdra is untruth'.
[3] VIII. 413.

labour was not dignified...... Similarly the karmakāra, the lakṣan, the carmaṇṇa or tanner, the weaver and others, quite dignified occupations in the *Ṛgveda*, are reckoned as Śūdras in the Pali texts (Fick, 160, 210)". It is evident that in the early tribal days some of the classes, that enjoyed a better status, became degraded as the tribes were advancing towards the feudal stage of development. In feudal society everywhere in the world labour is branded as undignified; hence all professions connected with manual labour become degraded in society. It was in this manner that some of the vocational classes that had enjoyed respectable status during the vedic period came to be regarded as Śūdras, i.e. servile castes, during the post-vedic and smṛti periods.

At places we find that the position of the Śūdras is not so lowly as in later times. In a few passages of the *Śatapatha Brāhmaṇa*[1] the Śūdra is given a place in the Soma-sacrifice. The early texts allude to such Śūdras and the authority of the *Maitrāyanī Saṁhitā*[2] and the *Pañcavaṁśa Brāhmaṇa*[3] may be cited in this regard. The *Śatapatha Brāhamaṇa*[4] mentions Śūdras as some of kings' ministers. The *Taittirīya Saṁhitā*[5] registers prayers for glory on behalf of Śūdra and other castes. The desire to be dear to Śūdra as well as to the Āryas is expressed in the *Atharvaveda*[6] and the *Vājasaneya Saṁhitā*[7]. Likewise the Sūtras[8] recognize that Śūdras can be merchants, or that they can even exercise any trade.[9]

But the later lot of the Śūdras is one of progressive deterioration, of unrelieved and unmitigated misery. Throughout the succeeding centuries their distinction centres round owe. From the *Sūtras* of Gautama, Baudhāyana and Āpastamba down to the commentaries and glosses of Kullūka Bhaṭṭa and Raghunandana one unqualified refrain is that of suppressed rights and exacted duties, and the burden wears down to the present day. The Śūdra is called the child of misery and his name is made synonimous with 'one who grieves', which phrase again spells the etymology of his privation. His numbers swell—the Sūtras and Dharmaśāstras enumerate them

[1] V. 5, 4, 9; I. 1, 4, 12. [2] IV. 2, 7, 10. [3] VI. 1, 11.
[4] V. 3, 22. [5] V. 7, 6, 4. [6] XIX, 348, 141.
[7] XVI 2. [8] *Gautama.*, X. 62. [9] *Viṣṇu.*, II. 14.

in positive scores and implied hundreds but numbers multiplied and multiplying fail to assuage the tension of his inequities and during the centuries that follow it is apparently the one endeavour of the Smṛtikāras to run down the Śūdras, to shear them of all physical and spiritual possessions and thus make them lick the dust. Manu weighs the scale aloft to the skies and completes their ruin. The most venerable cuts the cruellest and the wrong passes remedy. All Dharmaśātstra writers start with the presumption that all the *varṇas*—Brāhmaṇa, Kṣatriya, Vaiśya and Śūdra—are arranged in a descending order and that the last is the downmost.

The Code of Manu stands at the end of a line and in order to understand the implications of its constituents and commandments it is essential to trail along that line back to the beginnings. The celebrated Code is but the consummation of the social genesis and the end of a chain of which the links have been forged along the growth of centuries reflected in the corresponding literary and scriptural compositions. And it will not be only relevant to our purpose to study this social completion as embodied in the *Manusmṛti* along its channels of growth but the method will in addition seek to answer or at least to analyse, the vexed question of the origin of the Śūdras and other lower castes. The pan-Germanic myth of a nordic invasion (We do not question the theory of Aryan invasion of India) conquering and enslaving aboriginal ethnic units and thus creating castes has assumed such questionable proportions and gained such notoriety that the entire problem of the origin of the Śūdras has to be reopened and studied from new angles supported by the wealth of modern social sciences as against the defunct and obsolete nineteenth century socio-historical dogmas. And hence this discussion in certain detail of the origin of the Śūdras which incidentally affords a clue to the origin of the mixed castes, the pariahs and untouchables and the numerous Aspṛśyās and Antyajas who together number in hundreds and with whose declamation the pages not only of Manu's Code but of the Dharmasūtras and Smṛtis are crowded. We now pass on to the treatment of the same mixed castes and untouchables beside the Śūdras.

CHAPTER III

ŚUDRAS

Manu follows the Śruti

The *Manusmṛti* continues the burden of the *Ṛgveda* with regard to the *Varṇas* and thus establishes its *Smṛti* character of following the *Śruti*. It even partially reproduces the expression of the *Ṛgveda*[1] through its phrase '*mukhabāhurupādataḥ Brāhmaṇān Kṣatriyān Vaiśyān Śūdrānśca*[2] while enumerating the castes. Following the *Śruti* again it accepts only four castes and while doing so unequivocally declares that there is not a fifth caste beyond the additional four, *nāsti tu pañcamaḥ*.[3]

The enumeration is in the descending order and the caste preceding one takes precedence over it and over those following it in every thing. The Śūdra comes last of all and Manu does not mince matters while declaring that the three upper castes among the Varṇas are Dvijātis twice-born, by virtue of their second birth through *saṃskāras* and that the Śūdras are Ekajātis,[4] once-born, due to their want of right to initiation. The distinction, however, is one social and has nothing to do with stock or extraction for the Śūdra finds his place among the Varṇas, howsoever low, and the stigma arises from his lowly position in the order of the castes.

The Brahman, however, is the pick of the bunch. It is for him almost that all creation creates and acts. He not only heads the list of castes but is declared 'in all justice (*dharmataḥ*) the lord of this entire creation',[5] and lord of the Varṇas due to the performance of a special rite[6] (*saṁskāra*). He may or may not be 'learned' (*avidvānśca vidvānśca*), he all the same and veritably is a 'great god' (*daivataṁ-mahat*)[7].

1 *Brāhmaṇcasya mukhamāsīt*, etc., X. 90, 12.
2 *Manu*, I. 31. 3 X. 4. 4 Ibid.
5 सर्वस्यैवास्य सर्गस्य धर्मतो ब्राह्मणः प्रभुः ।। Ibid., I. 93.
6 संस्कारस्य विशेषाच्च वर्णानां ब्राह्मणः प्रभुः ।। Ibid, X.
7 Ibid., IX. 317.

And thus being *parama daivata* (great god), the 'Brahmans are to be reverenced'[1] (lit. worshipped).

This avowed declaration of the Varṇas being 'four and four alone' and refusing to accept a fifth one, Manu follows up by stigmatizing the rest of the humanity as barbarians living beyond the pale of civilization. "Whoever in this world are beside (beyond) those born of the mouth, arms, thighs and the feet (of Brahma)", he avers, "whether they speak the Aryan or non-Aryan (*mleccha*) tongue, they all without exception have been termed Dasyus".[2] Śūdras thus are beyond the range of the Dasyus[3] (the mixed castes and the Untouchables like the Cāṇḍālas), probably partly and indirectly implying even a non-Aryan descent being included among the basic four castes.

Authorities of Manu

In this regard Manu is not alone for all writers on Dharmaśāstra start with the proposition that the four Varṇas, Brāhmaṇa, Kṣatriya, Vaiśya and Śūdra are arranged in a descending scale of social status. Smṛti-writers try to place all their dicta in the frame work of the Varṇas because the four Varṇas and their duties and privileges had been more or less clearly defined during the times of the Vedas and the Brāhmaṇas, which too according to the authors of the Smṛtis were Śruti, eternal and infallible. They tried to approximate the state of society existing in their times to the Varṇas which they held were of hoary antiquity. Manu himself is not only no exception to this rule but is further more concentrated in his like convictions and avowals. He, however, many a time finds his authorities in the past at least in generality if not in specific cases.

If in order to understand Manu better we refer to literature composed prior to him we shall find that howsoever partisan he might seem with regard to the Śūdras, he is by no chance solitary in his mode of approach. In fact the composer of the Puruṣa hymn himself appears to regard the division of society into four classes as very ancient and as natural and divinely ordained as the sun and the moon. Indeed the idea

[1] सर्वथा ब्राह्मणाः पूज्याः परमं दैवतं हि तत् ॥ Ibid., 319.

[2] Ibid., X. 45.

[3] Cf. Ibid., V. 131.

gripped the mind of the early writers so tightly that the Saṁhitā,[1] the Brāhmaṇas[2] and the Upanishads[3], down to the *Mahābhārata*[4], carried this division right to the realm of gods and classified them in accordance with their castes. Thus Agni and Bṛhaspati became Brahmans among gods; Indra, Varuṇa, Soma and Yama Kshatriyas; Vasus, Rudras, the Viśvedevas and Maruts became Vaiśyas and Pūṣan became Śūdras. The classification in the *Mahābhārata* is slightly altered where Ādityas play the role of the Kshatriyas, Maruts of the Vaiśyas and Aśvins of the Śūdras.[5]

Manu's attitude towards the Vaiśyas and Śūdras, who are very often condemned or discriminated together in his Code, has its shape already set in the *Taittirīya Saṁhitā.*[6] It says : "The Vaiśya among men, cow among cattle, therefore they are to be enjoyed (to be eaten and subsisted upon) by others; they were produced from the receptacle of food, therefore they exceed others in numbers". The Śūdra finds his due place in the summary dispensation of the sage. "The Śūdra among men and horse among animals; therefore those two, the horse and the Śūdra, are the conveyances of beings; therefore the Śūdra is not fit (ordained) for sacrifice".[7]

Manu is fanatically hard on Śūdras. His hatred for them is unbounded. The class hatred of the *Manusmṛti*, composed most probably as the gospel of the great counter-revolution led by Puṣyamitra Śuṅga (the disciple of Patañjali and the supplanter of the heterogenous elements and non-Brahman line of rulers), for the lower castes and Untouchables as also for heterodox sects is too glaring to remain unnoticed. K. P. Jayaswal admits in his *Manu And Yājñavalkya* that the "Mānava Code thus suffers from its political, social and sacredotal prejudices", and that "this seems to have been the basis of the high authority it soon acquired. This rapidity in its acceptance is also due to probable royal recognition...Very

[1] *Maitrāyanī Saṁhitā,* I. 10. 13.

[2] *Śatapatha Br.*, XIV. 4, 2, 23-25; *Kauśītaki Br.*, IX. 5; *Aitareya Br.*, 35, 5.

[3] *Bṛhadāraṇyaka Upa.*, I. 4, 11-13.

[4] Śānti Parva, 208, 23-25.

[5] Ibid.

[6] VII. 1, 1, 5.

[7] Ibid., 1, 1, 6.

probably the *Mānava Dharma* code became the approved code of the Śungan regime".

Types of Śūdras

Manu's use of the term 'Śūdra' is both general and specific. Many a time he refers to them disparagingly in a general way to include those that belonging normally to the three upper castes have deteriorated throuth non-performance of duties and rites attaching to their castes,[1] those who have fallen to that status through marriage[2], those who have taken to the professions generally pursued by Śūdras[3] and those again who belong altogether to the mixed and untouchable classes who are outcastes, even pariahs. The cast of these are rather throughout vaguely termed as Śūdras. The specific reference to the term is in respect of those who are natural Śūdras born of Śūdra parents and belonging to the fourth and lowest main division of the four castes. It is mainly of this cast that we shall treat in this chapter. The mixed castes and the untouchables we shall take up in the next. Of course references to the rest also may sometime become an exegency of treatment.

The *Manusmṛti* makes at one place a sharp division between the free and the slave (dāsa) Śūdras.[4] In the beginning the reference is general where Manu says that the Śūdra is created to serve (literally to slave), but it becomes clear and pointed when he alludes to the 'bought' (*krīta*) and free[5] (*akrīta,* unbought) kinds of them. Of these the former could be freed[6] (*misṛṣṭah,* liberated) by his master. The difference between the two was that the saleable kind of the Śūdra served his master as his chattel and could be sold and bought at will and that the act of changing masters or choosing of vocations was not of his free will while the free kind of Śūdra, or for that matter even the 'liberated' kind could opt out in accordance with his wish and choice and could not be compelled to continue to serve the same master. Of course one thing was

[1] *Kriyālopādimah,* X. 43; (where Brahman ignorant of Veda labours for livelihood) II. 168; IV. 245; VIII. 16; XI. 24; XI. 97.

[2] III. 15-19.

[3] II. 168; also cf. many *anulomajas*; X. 65, 66, 92, 97, etc.

[4] *Dāsyam* IX. 413; also cf. ibid., 410. [5] Ibid., 413. [6] Ibid., 414.

common to both, the act of service[1] from which there was no emancipation. That was *Jātadharma*, the duty that he had inherited and as long as he stayed in the body politic he had to continue to perform that part of his implied contract. As pointed out elsewhere (above), however, Manu clearly puts this kind of *prakṛt*, natural, Śūdras apart from the Dasyus among whom most of the mixed castes are classed, although he does not discountenance the Dāsa type of Śūdras who could have been saleable slaves. This fact is sought to be particularly noted here to show that the Dāsas and Dasyus who were once reckoned among the local (partly aboriginal) enemies of the Rigvedic Aryans do not any more, not at any rate in the *Manusmṛti*, wear that characteristic. Dasyus have come to mean in the Mānava connotation some of the various Untouchables, the pariahs, some such other tribes also who had taken to criminal habits as a class and to some extent even conformed to the terms classical acceptation of the nobler, while Dāsas had broken away from their old association with the Dasyus and were now mere servants or slaves of which the latter again conform to the classical sense. The racial idea that originally embodied the term had now long dropped out and had even taken in Manu the simple sense of 'service' (*dāsyam*)[2] besides that of the restricted slave, *krīta* or *akrīta*.

Among the Kshatriya tribes that had in course of time through non-performance of *saṁskāras* or Dvija-rites succumbed to the degraded castes of the Śūdras are enumerated the following : Pauṇḍrakas, Draviḍas, Kambojās, Yavanas, Śakas, Pāradas, Prabhavas, Cinas, Kirātas, Daradas, and Khasas.[3] With regard to these we need hardly say that the condemnation of these peoples to the Śūdra rank from the Kshatriya status is arbitrary for we know that they were never Kshatriyas in the Smṛti sense but without doubt ethnic units independent of the Indian caste system. They had certainly been once the lords of the various localities of India which they had come to own in consequence of their conquest, which aspect although it may have lain in distant subconscious memory of Manu, is here, nevertheless, completely thrown overboard by the eminent law-giver. These enumerated tribes, as would be

1 Ibid., 410, 413. 2 Ibid. 3 Ibid., X. 43-45.

evident to students of history and ethnology were drawn from numerous independent stocks and besides the autochthons Draviḍas and various frontier clans and peoples represented the Greeks, Scythians, Persians and the Chinese. Strangely enough two among these, the Khasas[1] and the Draviḍas,[2] are further reckoned among the mixed castes, those born of the Kṣatriya and the Vrātya *savarṇa*[3] wedlock. Likewise the Ābhīras, who once built up a mighty empire like the Śakas in the western and central India, have been classed by Manu[4] among the mixed castes. He says that Ābhīra is begotten by a Brahman father on an Ambaṣṭa woman while an Ambaṣṭa is himself (or herself) begotten by a Brahman on a Vaiśya woman.[5] This enumeration, we humbly point out, is not scientific.

A fairly good crop is mentioned of those Śūdras who arose as a result of moral lapses, as for example where the caste Hindus appropriated or married Śūdra women. Of course there were many methods which contributed to the growth of the numbers and sub-castes of the Śūdras, one of them being these supposed ill-assorted unions. These did not only create Śūdras incidentally but even redounded in effect on the sinning fathers who were degraded by such contacts.[6] Manu not only does not approve of such unions but is singularly vehement in his condemnation of such defaulters.[7] If at all and ever he has to accept these it is more or less in the nature of continuing a burden descended on him from previous law-givers. It is more or less for that reason and for the sake of recounting and detailing the numerous and diverse mixed castes and Untouchables in the contemporaneous society that he lists their alarming types and sections, their duties and professions, their actions producing reactions and taboos among the caste Hindus, and their forbidding even helpless vicissitudes. He is honest at least to himself in his uncompromising attitude to the caste laxities and he calls upon the king to check such lapses and to maintain the keeping of the caste rules in society.[8] His condemnation of the Brahman, creating

[1] Ibid., 22. [2] Ibid. [3] Ibid. Also cf. ibid., 20.
[4] X. 15. [5] Ibid., 8, [6] III. 15-19 etc.
[7] Ibid., cf. also the context of penalties and *prāyaścitta* following.
[8] X. 61.

such lapses himself is relentless although the main burden falls on the wretched and unfortunate Śūdra for, since having completely identified himself with the interests of the all-powerful and nonetheless materialist Brahman, Manu makes the Śūdra and his lowly associates to bear the brunt and visits them with all the unrelenting privations which in all justice should have been the penalty of the erring Brahman.

Before discussing further the types and professions of the Śūdras we may return for a moment to the topic of the slave-Śūdra to allude to a few divisions of them mentioned in the *Manusmṛti*. The division of Śūdra proper is in seven classes[1] : 1 Conquered from enemy in war (Dhvajahṛtaḥ); 2 Bhakta-Dāsa, literally, devoted slave or servant, (the commentator explains the phrase as the 'servant who has come motivated with the greed of gain);[2] 3 Home-born (Gṛhajaḥ) whom the commentator explains as 'Son of a maid-servant or female slave' (Dāsīputraḥ); 4 Bought slave (Krīta); 5 One given by others (Datṛma): 6 Ancestral (Paitṛkaḥ); and 7 One recieved in lieu of compensation (Daṇḍadāsaḥ).

This classification will make it clear that all of these were not slaves nor mere servants either. But the nature of each can easily be determined. Dāsa, literally 'slave' in classical Sanskrit and in later other Indian vernaculars, has been used by Manu very often in a general sense to indicate a servant as also *dāsya* to denote service. But despite that basic implication which centres round service it also includes the work of those that are not mere servants but slaves. There can hardly be two opinions regarding the first of the seven, Dhvajahṛta, who positively was a slave taken prisoner in war from his master. The commentator is correct when he explains the phrase *sangrāmasvāmisakāśājjito*,[3] 'conquered from master's side in war'. Bhaktadāsa sounds like a servant who comes to serve his master for mere monitary gain and is like the usual modern household servant, a wage earner. Dāsīputra may have been either a simple servant born of a maid-servant or a slave born of a female slave. Dāsī could be both a maid-servant or a female slave. It is not clear, however, if this son is begotten on the Dāsī (maid-servant or the female slave) by the master, her

[1] VIII. 415. [2] *Bhaktālobhadyupagatadāsyo.*

[3] Comment on *Dhvajahṛta* in ibid. (VIII. 415).

own husband in case one was permitted, or by one of the many domestics. Any way, it is clear that this type of servant was raised at home on those already serving the master. There cannot be any other interpretation of the fourth kind, the *Krīta*, who was a slave bought by money. Slave markets were not unknown in India. Not only do the Greeks accompanying Alexander allude to them but even Kauṭilya registers them in his *Arthaśāstra*, that rare treatise on statecraft (almost contemporaneous in a number of incidents with the *Manusmṛti*) in which he distinguishes between Ārya-Śūdra and Anārya-Śūdra, servant and slave. Further, within a hundred years of the composition of the code of Manu an uncommon commercial document, the *Periplus of the Erythrean Sea*, recounts among its items of trade fair slaves that were brought from the west by dealers in slaves and sold in India as pieces of merchandise. The first of Manu's enumeration, Dvajahṛtaḥ, may not have been isolated example for wars were normal and captives taken were quite a few, (an Asokan Rock edict detailing the horrors of the Kalinga war only about a hundred years before the composition of the Code of Manu counts the spoils of captured men in a hundred and fifty thousand) and all could not have been appropriated by the conqueror. Several might have taken their place in the display of the market until an eye of favour and gold might have put an end to their unowned character by winning for them their due place among the proverbial 'bipeds and quadrupeds' for whom the Ṛigvedic bard had begged of the mighty heaven lasting weal (Mark the categorical expression of the ṛsi with regard to the wretched domestic and slave and the august company in which he is referred—द्विपदश्चतुष्पदः !

Thus *Krīta* was a slave bought with money as was one following it in the enumeration of Manu, *Datrima*, given. This was a gift of a friend or relation, even perhaps the part of a sumptuous dowry; but this last is a mere speculation for at least the text does not warrant it. The nature of this kind of employee almost settled the fact of his being made an item of gift. After all a gift in law can be good only when it was unencumbered and when the person making it had full ownership and possession over it. This could be so only when the reference is interpreted to mean a slave. The ancestral Dāsa again seems to have been a slave for to be hereditarily bound to a family and to form an item of its ancestral devolution one had to be a slave and not a mere domestic because the latter had the right to choose his master and calling and, at any rate, could opt out to a new and promising opening at will. The last of the seven was *Daṇḍadāsa*, received in lieu of compensation. We should not wonder if this kind of servant was a victim of misfortune and had been reduced to his state incidental to a mishap in gambling, usury or to a money penalty in law. All these three situations point in effect to a simple one, that of a debtor who could pay back his count and thus set off against his creditor by serving a term with him: Daṇḍadāsa was therefore only circumstantial servant.

Thus out of the seven kinds of Śūdra servants at least four appear to have been slaves who could be bought and sold at will. That is why Manu even permits a Brahman master to take away all wealth from his slave or servant without the fear of state prosecution, for the Śūdra (Dāsa, slave or servant in the present context) cannot in the very nature of things possess anything as his own, *na hi tasyāsti kiñcitsvam*, and is *Bhartṛhāryadhanaḥ*, capable of being dispossessed of his belongings by his master.[1] Kullūka Bhaṭṭa while commenting on this rare piece of social justice strengthens the Brahmanic privilege by elucidating the passage that 'Thus the Brahman taking away the property (or wealth or possessions), of Dāsa even forcibly in distress cannot be penalized by the king'.[2] The verse preceding that under review makes this interpretation abundantly clear by theorizing on the context. It says that Bhāryā, wife, Putra, son, and Dāsa, servant (slave), all the three for certain are decreed (dubbed, legislated-*smṛtaḥ*) 'property-less' (*adhanāḥ*) and that all that they earn belongs to one to whom they belong.[3] The fact of the Śūdra servant or slave being reckoned in the same line and breath of the wife and son does not in any measure mitigate the rigour of the decree for, in fact he is never the recepient of similar favours. The wife has identified herself with the interests of her husband

[1] VIII. 417.

[2] एवं चापदि बलादपि दासाद्ब्राह्मणो धनं गृह्णन्न राजा दण्डनीय इति—।

[3] *Manu.*, VIII. 416.

and has a stake in the home and a vested and deferred (although sometimes only a contingent) interest in her husband's property and the son is the potential heir to all that his father owns, but the wretched slave and the unfortunate servant has to toil without redemption, without the possiblities of betterment, devoid of hope.

Duties

Duties are in accordance with the *guṇas*, qualities, but not qualities in the sense of merits or personal attainments but those circumstanced by the actions of former births.[1] These *guṇas* constitute the nature of beings because they are the ruling factors of creation through the original matter (*prakṛti*). Prakṛti was even and formless in the sense of the Sānkhya characterization when the qualities therein were *sama*, in equipoise, but as they changed in measure prakṛti deteriorated from her original poise and lost her equillibrium thus giving shape to matter and ultimately to creation. These *guṇas* are three in number, *Sattva*, *Rajas*, and *Tamas*, respectively the bright, the energetic and the dark respectively again culminating in created forms of the divine human and lower beings like the birds.[2] The nature creating the Śūdra is desire-merited (*kāmapradhāna*), *tamas*, and naturally his entire outlook is thus constituted with irrepressible components engendering his sinful state, next only to the plants and static things, worms and insects, fishes, serpents and reptiles, tortoises, cattle and beasts,[3] and in the same line as elephants, horses, lions, tigers, boars and the sinful Mlecchas.[4] This *tamas* nature of the Śūdra must reflect his status in society and define his calling and the celebrated code nowhere slackens in its enthusiasm to give sacredotal one.

With respect to the status of the Brahman the act of serving others has been characterized as the 'dogs' living' (*śvavṛtti*)[5] and he has therefore been forbidden to adopt that ever as his calling.[6] But the same has been ordained for the Śūdra as the

[1] XII. 39, 52-54. [2] XII. 40., cf. also ibid., 38.
[3] Ibid., 42. [4] Ibid., 43.
[5] IV. 6; 4.
[6] न श्ववृत्त्या कदाचन ibid., 4.

natural, normal and only *dharma*, duty.[1] While the Brahman receives punishment[2] for making Kshatriyas and Vaiśyas serve him the Śūdra has to be compelled by the king to do his duty which is to serve others.[3] We have already cited elsewhere Manu's dictum that the Śūdra has been created by Svayambhū (Brahmā, the Creator) to serve the Brahman and other twice-born castes. To serve the learned Brahmans and famed householders is the sole duty of the Śūdra, producing merit and svarga.[4] By serving the Brahmans and the rest of the twice-born, in due order, after attaining bodily purity and with sweet words and devoid of arrogance the Śūdra attains to the status of higher castes in the following birth.[5]

While choosing his master a Śūdra's first preference must be the Brahman and in his absence alone should he proceed to serve the Kshatriya and, failing him, a rich Vaiśya.[6] The law-giver declares that the service of the Brahman alone is productive of immense merit, all other work is without any consequence.[7] Thus for the gains in this world and for mertis in the other the Brahman has to be served by the Śūdra. The very fact that he is under the tutelege of the Brahman should reassure him for in serving the Brahman he brings his actions to exhaustive fruition (*kṛtakṛtyatā*).[8] Acting in this manner does the Śūdra attain to lasting fame in this world.[9] His one work is sevice (*dāsyam*) and whether he is bought or unbought (*krīta* or *akrīta*) the Śūdra has to perform his duty, that of serving the Brahman for which he has been created by the creator.[10] A slave-Śūdra could be freed by his master if he so chose but the act of liberation could not free the slave from service, for service is Śūdra's *nisargaja*,[11] (natural) duty, his ordained *dharma*. Manu affirms that while the *tapas* (arduous duty) of the Brahman is *jñāna*, of the Kṣatriya is affording protection to others, of the Vaiśya is *vārtā* (agriculture, trade and cattle-raising), that of the Śūdra is *sevanam*,

[1] Manu refers to this any number of times as references following this will show.

[2] राज्ञा दण्ड्यः शतानि षट् ibid., VIII. 412.

[3] Ibid., 418.

[4] Ibid., IX. 334.

[5] Ibid., 335.

[6] Ibid., X. 121.

[7] Ibid., 123.

[8] Ibid., 122.

[9] Ibid., 127.

[10] Ibid., VIII. 413.

[11] Ibid., 424.

service.[1] That is Śūdra's natural avocation which det·:rmines his status.

This status of the Śūdra one of universal service of the twice-born, is so patent with the law-givers that Manu and other Smṛtikāras following him find easy authority for their bias against the Śūdra in anterior literature. The *Aitareya Brāhmaṇa* remarks that the Śūdra is at the beck and call of others (i.e. the three upper *varṇas*), he can be made to rise at will, he can be beaten at will.[2] *The Tāṇḍya Mahābrāhmaṇa* says that the Śūdra does not go beyond washing the feet (of the twice-born), since he was created from the feet.[3] Strengthened with such high authorities Manu naturally does not fight shy of the inequities, social injustice and discriminations with which he has condemned the Śūdra. He even threatens him in consequence of default in conforming to his ordained duty with the after death fate of an incubus that feeds on filthy worms.[4] The reference, however, occurs along the penalties declared for lapses in performing duties by other castes also.

The status of the Śūdras as inferred from the duties enjoined on them can further be guessed from the professions he practised and the vocations he pursued. This aspect of our discussion will shed further light on the types and varieties of the Śūdras. Hence we now pass on to the topic of the professions followed by them.

Professions

In modern times gains in particular callings ensure public status. In early times it was more or less the castes and duties attaching to them that determined the social status of an individual. There is no doubt, however, and we have said that elsewhere in no equivocal terms that ultimately, originally and in the last analysis in those ancient days it was the profession which conditioned a man's status in society. It was because of this that the Śūdras and pariahs had come to an inglorious and unenviable social condemnation. Ser-

[1] ब्राह्मणस्य तपो ज्ञानं तपः क्षत्रस्य रक्षणम् ।
वैश्यस्य तु तपो वार्ता तपः शूद्रस्य सेवनम् ॥ ibid., XI. 235.

[2] Kane : *History of Dhaımaśāstra*, II. P. 35.

[3] Ibid., P. 34.

[4] *Manusmṛti*, XII. 72.

vice had soiled them and once they had fallen to their obnoxious state there was nothing to save them for Hinduism keeps only a debit account and seldom credits those back to their original status who have for the sins of others or their own accepted as their lot even once.

Several professions, besides the service of the twice-born, have been considered in certain cirucumstances fit for the Śūdras while followers of certain others have been generally termed as Śūdras. The professions referred to in the Code of Manu, and they are quite a few in number, reveal not only as to what the Śūdras and other castes could or should pursue as a vocation but also a state of society which, having broken away from its primitive moorings, had, inspite of the scriptural orthodoxy and its static rôle, chosen to be dynamic and had created and recreated patterns of diverse pursuits.[1] Social life is generally shaped by political interests which themselves are but a projection of the contempraneous economic structure. This economic structure is the outcome of the multiple economic activities in which professions to keep life in tact and to live better play their prominent part. The *Manusmṛti* in course of discussing its topics refers to a good number of them although in the interest of the arrangement of our data it will not be possible to enumerate them here. A reference to them is bound to be of a limited character for, firstly, we have circumscribed our discussion to the state of the Śūdra and other lower castes and the various callings of the twice-born are naturally ruled out; secondly, this being a treatment restricted to the Śūdras alone the vocations of the mixed castes, the outcastes, the untouchables and the pariahs do not find a place here. This latter aspect of the soicio-economic structure may form the subject of discussion of a subsequent chapter of this dissertation.

We have already referred to the fallen caste-men. Those that fell from a former enviable status indeed fell to a ground where social decorum could not be practised and, instead, ways and means had to be found to sustain the body. The Brahmans alone, since the subject of legislation was more or less, in fact more than less, their concern and privilege,

[1] *Śilpāni vividhāni*, *Manu.*, X. 100.

could claim their sustenance comparatively easily from the community, others had to devise means to procure their livelihood. And as conforming to the mere principles of avocations of the four castes could never govern the ever-growing potentiality of the mass of men they were bound to look for grub far beyond the narrow limits of a priestly sociocraft.

Besides the Śūdras profession as a domestic or errand boy (*preṣya*), others also find mention in Manu which could be pursued by them. A good number of these pursuits may have been the exlusive monopoly of the mixed castes and the untouchables and we shall deal with them in due context. There were those followed by the Śūdras too although allusions to them in the code are rather vague.

It seems that the Śūdra could employ himself as a tailor (*tunnavāya*),[1] literally needle-worker, blacksmith (*karmāra*)[2] which the commentator explains with the word *lauhakāra*,[3] goldsmith (*suvarṇakāra*),[4] and maker of baskets (*kāruka*[5]= *sūpakāra*, which can also mean a cook of soup) which profession is permitted to Śūdra only as an *āpaddharma* or a calling pursued in distress when no course to follow the normal profession has remained open.[6] Allied were the professions of workers in bamboo (*veṇakāra*),[7] which today has become a concern of one of the mixed castes, dealer in arms (*śastravikrayī*),[8] and of the wine brewer (śauṇḍika).[9] Most of these occur in connection with the Śūdras or castes whose cooked food the Brahman should avoid eating for that contaminates him by unsettling his own character as a Brahman as also by affecting his nature, fame and age. Some of these may well have formed professions of the Vaiśyas and some have degenerated as callings exclusively pursued by the untouchables to-day. There were those others that should have been more logically the professions of Vaiśyas according to the broad principles of the caste system as enunciated by Manu but that are mentioned in connection with the vocations of the Śūdras. These were the tiller of the soil, the ploughman (*ardhika*),[10] one who tended the cattle (*gopāla*,[11] *gorakṣa*,)[12]

[1] *Manu*, IV. 214. [2] bid., 215. [3] Vide comment on ibid.
[4] Ibid., 215, 218. [5] Ibid., 219; VII. 138; VIII. 65; 102; X. 100.
[6] Ibid., X. 99. [7] Ibid., IV. 215. [8] Ibid., 215-220.
[9] Ibid., IX. 225; IV. 216. [10] Ibid., IV. 253. [11] Ibid. [12] Ibid., 102.

barber (*nāpita*)[1], artisans and craftsmen in general that among others might have included the *śilpīs*[2] like the various smiths and masons, and dyers (and cleaners, *rañjaka*).[3] Manual labourers (*ātmopajīvinaḥ*[4] whom the commentator explains as Śūdras—Śūdrān is mentioned in the original test itself[5]—*dehakleśopajīvino bhārikādin*)[6] were beside the domestic servants and they appear to have gained their liveliğhood like now by executing the various needs of the householders without being all time servants. They might have done job or piece work. They along with the *śilpins* or craftsmen have been mentioned among them, from whom the king could claim a day's work in the month.[7] A few professions have been indirectly hinted at by condemning the Brahman pursuing them as being Śūdras' callings were considered derogatory to his status. These were the following : the crafts (*śilpa*)—various arts of painting, carving, *citrakarmādi*, as explained by the commentator,[8] to which list the work of the potter, wood-carver, musical instrument maker, and of the like may be added), commercial relations by use of capital (*vyavahāra* expalained by commentator as *dhanaprayogātmaka*, may be lending business or usury), purchase and sale of cows (cattle in general), horses and chariots (including perhaps carts or bullock-carts, *yānaiḥ*) and agriculture.[9] Obviously since all Vaiśyas were not agriculturists or landowners and tradesmen, as all Kshatriyas were not warriors or all Brahmans priets, many of the Vaiśyas' duties might in course of time have taken over as pursuits by others. Looking after the cattle, which might include even their ownership and rearing as also tilling of the land which again might have at times become plots in possession, were some of the callings that had descended to the Śūdras. Manu a time, as alluded elsewhere, the Vaiśayas and Śūdras have been referred to together and jointly by Manu. In the present context and with regard to the professions just mentioned the Brahmans were profiteers although Manu enumerates

[1] Ibid., IV. 253. [2] Ibid., VII. 138; 111, 64. X. 100. There were numerous *śilpas* (*śilpāni vividhāni*).

[3] Ibid., IV. 216. [4] Ibid., VII. 138.

[5] शूद्राश्चात्मोपजीविन: ibid. [6] Vide comment on ibid.

[7] एकैकं कारयेत्कर्म मासि मासि महीपति: ibid., VII. 138.

[8] Comment on *Manu.*, III. 64. [9] *Manu.*, ibid.

them in that connection only to forbid them as pursuits fit for a Brahman.[1] In another instance,[2] that of the acceptability of evidence in a court of law, Manu expects a Brahman witness to be treated as a Śūdra (*śūdravadācaret*) who pursued the calling of a cowherd (*gorakṣa*), trader or shopkeeper (*vaṇijika*), cook of soup (*kāru*, perhaps maker of baskets), domestic or errand boy (*preṣya*), or of an actor or rope-dancer (*vardhasika*, elsewhere *śailūsa*[3] or *naṭa*: living by *naṭakarma*, i.e., dancing and singing, *nṛtyagītādijīvniaḥ*, commentator).[4] Since the pursuit of the above named professions compel the law courts to treat a Brahman like a Śūdra it is obvious that these had become natural avocations of the Śūdras despite Manu's traditional approach to the *varṇadharma*. These were therefore callings legitimately pursued by both the Brahman and the Śūdra, legitimate because the Brahman is not punishable for that in law, only his privilege, which in normal course would have been considerable is sought to be dropped out of being accorded. Elsewhere (quoted a member of times before and after) the Brahman is socially chastized for his change of profession. This enumeration incidently also adds trade (*vāṇijya*)[5] and acting, dancing and singing (*vardhusika*,[6] *śailūṣa* and *kuśīlava*)[7] to the number of professions, that the Śūdra pursued. Weavers (*tantuvāya*) was another profession to which Manu[8] alludes but we are not sure if this was a calling for the Śūdras or for the untouchables. Just as a distinction has been made between a slave-servant (*dāsa*) and domestic or errand boy (*bhṛtaka*, *preṣya*)[9] so also is a distinction made between the printing and dying of cloth. Boths a cloth-printer (*raṅgāvatarka*)[10] and dyer (*rañjaka*)[11] have been mentioned. The profession of both may have been the concern of the same man as now, as the context in which they have been mentioned shows.[12] *Niṣāda*[13] catcher of fish,[14] has found mention as a mixed caste but they were untouchables although they are not so to-day.

[1] Ibid., 63-65.
[2] Ibid., VIII. 102.
[3] Ibid., IV. 214. Also *kuśīlava* cf. ibid.. VIII. 65; 102.
[4] Comment on ibid., VIII. 102.
[5] Ibid.
[6] Ibid., VIII. 102.
[7] Ibid., 397.
[8] दासेन भृतकेन वा ibid., VIII. 70. प्रेष्य ibid., 102.
[9] Ibid., IV. 215.
[10] Ibid., 216
[11] Cf. ibid., 215, 216.
[12] Ibid., 215. X. 48.
[13] मत्स्यघातः ibid., X. 48.
[14] Ibid., X. 92.

The Brahman has been permitted indirectly to pursue trade although the direct injuction is against it. Among the articles of trade forbidden for the Brahman to sell are meat, lac, salt, *tryaha* (perhaps *hing*, but it is not quite clear) and milk. The sale of these five items of merchandise, says Manu, would presently reduce a Brahman to the state of a Śūdra thus indicating indirectly that the above named commodities could be dealt in by a Śūdra. The implication is supported by the following verse which suggests that dealing in other articles would reduce a Brahmaṇ to the caste of a Vaiśya (*Vaiśyabhāvam niyacchati*), as against the *Śūdrabhāva* (*Śūdro bhavati brāhmaṇaḥ*).

There is positive injunction against the Śūdra, and other lower castes taking to higher castes' professions and in order to keep the *status quo* of the Code even the king's pressure and penalty have been invoked by our eminent authority. Manu suggests that the king should reduce to abject poverty (by forfeiting everything) a member of the low castes and exile him forthwith if he engages due to greed in a livlihood usually followed by one of the upper castes.[1] But despite such threats there were instances where the Śūdra at times attempted a break-away from his lowly state by pursuing others' trade and as will be shown later, even amassed wealth enough to arouse the cupidity of others. Besides others one reference[2] countenances a situation in which a servant (*bhṛtaka*=*dāsa*) could be both a teacher (*adhyāpaka*) and a pupil (*adhyāpita*) as also a Śūdra could be both a pupil (*śiṣya*) and teacher (*guru*) and in consequence could talk inagreeably boldly (*vāgduṣṭa*). He has been even penalised for preaching to the Brahmans arrogantly.[3] This settles the fact that, howsoever sparse, the occasions were not entirely unkown when the Śūdra could make bold and arrogate to himself the act of scriptural study so as to be further hated and denounced with decrees.

The usual openings for the Śūdra besides his *dāsyakarma*, act of serving, were multiple, like the profession of *kāruka*

[1] यो लोभादधमो जात्या जीवेदुत्कृष्टकर्मभिः ।
तं राजा निर्धनं कृत्वा क्षिप्रमेव प्रवासयेत ॥ ibid., 96.

[2] Ibid., III. 156.

[3] Ibid., IV. 61.

and the sphere of various *śilpas*, crafts, (*śilpāni vividhāni*)[1] to which he could be taken himself, but the ruling factor there too has to be service of the twice-born, as while choosing these consideration was expected to be had of the fact that the choice was conducive to the gain of the *Dvijātis* (twice-born).[2] The Śūdra, burdened by wife and children and thus distressed by hunger, not normally able to serve the twice-born, is permitted to take professions like the *kāruka's*.[3] This exception could give the Śūdra a veritable footing and, getting bold by the corrupting and desparing inequities, both social and legal, he could rebel in desparation against his exploiters and bid for power. It is not without reason that even after the fall of the Śūdra Nandas only over a century prior to the composition of the *Manusmṛti* there ruled in India numerous families of Śūdra extraction. Even this celebrated Code of Manu knows of and alludes to Śūdra kings and forbids the twice-born to reside in his domain.[4] The injunction is scathing and sweeping. Nothing could be so derogatory to the Śūdras, the untouchables and to the heterodox sects like the Buddhism and others than the contents of this verse.

[1] Ibid., X. 100. Both Gautama (X. 62) and Viṣṇu (:1.14) permit Śudra to be merchants and the latter gives him the rig t to pursue all trades.

[2] Ibid. [3] Ibid., 99.

[4] न शूद्रराज्ये निवसेन्नाधार्मिकजनावृते ।
न पाषण्डिगणाक्रान्ते नोपसृष्टेऽन्त्यजैर्नृभिः ॥ ibid., IV. 61.

CHAPTER IV

SOCIAL AND ECONOMIC STATUS

Social

From the foregoing pages it will be evident that from the days of the *Ṛgveda* down to those of the *Manusmṛti* and later the lot of the Śūdra like that of woman has gone on worsening. The *Manusmṛti* gave almost its final seal to the misfortune of the Śūdras and other lowly castes.

Śūdra is theoretically sprung up from the same *puruṣa* and should have the same duties and rights as the rest of the four *varṇas* but his lot has not been only uneven but positively wretched and he has stood through the past centuries on the lowest rung of the ladder without the advantages of the rung. In every field of social activity he is branded as a lesser human entity and everywhere he is made to work to the advantage of others.

All kinds of indignities are hurled against him, every kind of discrimination is his poor lot. Even in such a common place for instance as naming he is to be slighted, for whereas the Brahman's name has to sound auspicious (*māṅgalyam*), the Kshatriya's valaint and the Vaiśya's has to indicate wealth, the Śūdra's name has to express slander, *jugupsā*[1] (*nindāvācakam dīnanāmānam*[2], the Commentator). Śūdra thus had to bear a very name indicating privation and slander and debased status. The following verse makes his position still more unbearable. It suggests discriminatory *upapadas*, surnames to the castes, and as usual the Śūdra finds his surname reflecting further privation. The Brahman should use 'Śarman' for his surname, the Kshatriya 'Varman' indicating his prowess and protection, the Vaiśya likewise reflecting prosperity but the Śūdra must bear a surname pronouncing condemnation on him. This should be indicative of his status of a *preṣya*,

[1] Ibid., II. 31.

[2] Comment on ibid.

servant.[1] he *Yamasmṛti* almost repeats the condemnation.[2] The *Viṣṇu Purāṇa* likewise supports Manu.[3] The Brahman becomes pure during *ācamana* by water reaching his heart, the Kshatriya by water crossing the throat, the Vaiśya by water reaching that region but the Śūdra immediately as the water touches the tongue and the lips.[4] In simple etiquette too a marked distinction is maintained.[5] Besides, he is not saluted at all.[6] Following Āpastamba,[7] Manu prescribes a different formula for asking welfare on meeting a Śūdra, that of 'health' (*ārogya*).[8] This also embodies a slur for that indirectly brings to the fore his duty to serve for to that most conducive would be a strong and healthy body. He could be shown some respect only when he grew beyond ninety which must have been a rare age even in the days of Manu.

Śūdras and women came in course of time to have similar rights and were generally grouped together[9] by Hindu law-givers. Manu has repeatedly done so. Manu does it more frequenty than others which shows the constantly deteriorating position of both, but, as said above, the more lamentable lot of the two was that of the Śūdra because relief never came to him, not even in old age, not even through his progeny. Likewise the Vaiśyas too many a time came to be reagarded with the same indifference as the Śūdras, and were subjected to similar indignities. We have quoted apt and ample instances elsewhere to show the proximity of the two. Indeed only the first two of the four varṇas—the Brahman and the Kshatriya—had an agreeable compromise between them and they already were acting in the manner suggested by the laterly *Bhaṭṭikāvyam*, *Kṣātradvijatvaṁ ca parasparārtham*, the Brahman and the Kshatriya have to grow their interests and gains through mutual assistance.

1 शूद्रस्य प्रेष्यसंयुतम् ibid., 32.

2 शर्मदेवश्च विप्रस्य वर्मत्राता च भूभुजः ।
भूतिदत्तश्च वैश्यस्य दासः शूद्रस्य कारयेत ॥

3 शर्मवद्ब्राह्मणस्योक्तं वर्मेति क्षत्रसंयुतम् ।
गुप्तदासात्मकं नाम प्रशस्तं वैश्यशूद्रयोः ॥

4 *Manu.*, II. 62. 5 Ibid., 125. 6 Ibid., 126.

7 कुशलमवरवयसं समानवयसं वा विप्रं पृच्छेत् ।
अन्नामयं क्षत्रियं क्षेमं वैश्यं आरोग्यं शूद्रम् ॥

8 *Manu.*, II. 127. 9 223.

While the twice-born have to choose between land and land for their habitat as stigma attached to their settling down in certain localities considered impure but since the Śūdra was too lowly to be affected by regional impurity, he was permitted to live wherever he liked.[1] Oridinarily he was rendered devoid of all *Dvijakarma.*[2] The Śūdra's sight had to be avoided during the time of offering oblations. He should neither see nor be seen by the *Yajamān* while the *homa* ceremony was in progress, for his very proximity pollutes the act.[3] In that context he has been classed with the hvar, the cock, the lame and the one-eyed.[4] Contrary to this principle even a begging Brahman (*bhikṣukam vāpi*) has to be accorded deep reverence.[5] During the obsequies (the *śrāddha* ceremony he and the like of him (*dāsavarga*),[6] and in this regard all the domestic servants, slaves and manual workers may have been meant, were not to be fed even with the left-overs and the food fallen on the ground (*uccheṣaṇam bhūmigatam*). As a matter of fact the Śūdras have to be completely avoided at the Śrāddha feast and the injunction in this connection is so severe that the fate of the feeder of the Śūdras thereafter is of one who goes with his head downward to the terrible Kalasūtra hell.[7] It is further ordained that whosoever (Brahman) approaches a *Vṛṣalī*, Śudra woman, after eating śrāddha food shall render his dead ancestors (*pitaras*) extremely unhappy.[8] While observing a vow (*vrata*) a Śūdra must not be contacted or talked to.[9] During morning and evening as also at noon Śūdra's company has to be avoided.[10]

Since he is considered generally apart from the twice-born the Śūdra has been given his special *pitaras* called. *Sukālin.*[11] His *pitaras* are supposed, however, to have discended from Vasiṣtha[12] which fact will incidentally strengthen our remark made before that the Śūdras have not to be taken to represent a race different from the Aryans.

1 Ibid., II. 24.

2 शूद्रवद्बहिष्कार्यः सर्वस्माद्द्विजकर्मणः ibid., 103.

3 Ibid., III. 239-42.

4 Ibid., 239, 242.

5 Ibid., 243.

6 Ibid., 246.

7 Ibid., 249.

8 Ibid., 250.

9 Ibid., XI. 223.

10 Ibid., IV. 140.

11 Ibid. III. 197.

12 Ibid., 198.

In point of *ātithya* also Manu makes a distinction in the status of the castes. It is clear from a verse[1] that only a man of a higher class can really be termed an *atithi*, 'venerable stranger,' and not the vice versa. For example, a Brahman or a Kshatriya alone could be an *atithi* at the house of a Kshatriya and not a Vaiśya or Śūdra. Likewise any of the lower three *varṇas* could not be treated as an honoured guest *atithis* in the house of a Brahman. But provision has been made, however, for looking after a Vaiśya and a Śūdra stranger in case he appeared at a Brahman's house. In that case they have to be fed along with the servants (*bhṛtyaiḥ saha*)[2] of the family. This instance further stimulates our proposition that the Vaiśya's position was also deteriorating in society and, although in theory they are classed among the twice-born by Manu, their status was positively low and their real and normal rank in practice was with the Śūdras. Indcidentally, the Vaiśya's position too has been treated in Manu and anterior authorities with growing contempt. His profession is getting narrower and narrower so as to be reduced to the strictly commercial and to exclude the ownership of and the proprietory right in land, and, although in course of centuries at times his individual status due to his worshipful supplications (in the form of building temples and responding agreeably to the wishes and pleasures of the lord of the varṇas, *varṇānām prabhuḥ*) to the Brahman gains lustre he is never treated with deference either by Manu or by authorities on Dharma prior to him.

Regarding the *saṁskāras*, it must be admitted that the Śūdra was absolutely innocent of them. The entire structure of the social and caste status was based on them and it was in consequence of the right attaching to the performance of the *saṁskāras* that the Dvijātis—the three upper castes, the Brahman, Kshatriya and Vaiśya—acquired their name. They were called the twice-born, for after their natural nativity they had to undergo another, second spiritual or social birth which won for them their specific name as against one, the Śūdra and other lower castes, to whom the *saṁskāras* were denied. The attitude of the law-givers in this regard stiffens to such an extent that the indifference to the *saṁskāras* and growing slackness

[1] Ibid., 110. [2] Ibid., 112.

in regard to their performance renders even the Kshatriyas and Vaiśyas low and makes them lose their caste. Even the enumeration of the three traditional castes among the twice-born is affected in certain localities. And finally after the Muhammedan invasion we find Nāgabhaṭṭa of Mahārāṣṭra and Raghunandana of Bengal asserting and propagating the view that there were only two castes, the Brahman and the Śūdra, there was none third, and they degraded all the non-Brahmans to the status of the Śūdra. Madras and Southern India in general including the Deccan, and, as a matter of fact, all the regions lying beyond the Madhyadeśa, followed suit. In recent years consideration of the real nature of the castes based on the *saṁskāras* in relation to the claims of inheritance has again and again come up for hearing and determination before the High Courts of Judicature mainly in Madras and Bengal, and they have had to take decision whether there are only two castes, the Brahman and the Śūdra, or more. Even accepting the traditional theory of the *cāturvarṇya* it cannot be determined whether a man belongs to this caste or that for their basic feature, the *saṁskāras* themselves, has been absent and naturally the determination regarding a man's caste has to be now, as ever if at all, by birth for that settles the region of man both in point of time and in the circuit of relations. The growing number of the sub-castes and their sections and sub-sections were the necessary dialectical negation of the caste structure which spelt its dismemberment and consequent ruin, for the extent of growth of the divisions could not be, as in the nature of things it cannot be, conditioned or governed by the processes of the Dharma laws. The uncontrolled growth engendered lapses and laxities in the performance of the *saṁskāras* and that one specific, even single, feature of the castes became indeterminative and the result at places was a reviewing of the caste position by the mediaeval jurists and commentators like Nāgabhaṭṭa and Raghunandana and a total distinction of the two intermediate castes, the Kshatriyas and the Vaiśyas. There could not be any doubt regarding the border extremes—the Brahman and the Śūdras—for the former had stuck like a leech to the system of the caste rules and the latter had known no bounds. The days of Manu, however, were the days of the *saṁskāras*. It was besides the days of foreign barbarian inroads, barbarian in the correct juristic sense of the Indian scriptural legislation, which compelled the law-givers to clinch the caste rules further to save what had remained from alien ethnical infiltration. Manu's laws, mainly the *saṁskāras*, in consequence, in the sphere of social legislation, took a determined attitude laying emphasis on the caste rules and the *saṁskāras*. Hence the propriety of this discussion as a prelude to our study of *saṁskāras*, their mandates and denials.

A verse[1] in the *Manusmṛti* boldly denies *saṁskāras* to the Śūdra (*na saṁskāramarhati*), and in consequence of this fundamental denial other negative results naturally follow : 'The Śūdra does not commit a sin (by acting contrary to *dvijadharma*), has no right in Dharma (not now, but under the scriptural law the right to perform religious rights and ceremonies) and therefore no contrary rulings in Dharma affecting him (*na asyādhikāro dharme asti na dharmāt pratiṣedhanam*). It is a crucial fundamental verse denying the Śūdra the right to worship in the manner of the twice-born, denying his existence, as it were, in the righteousness, and since he is given no right of performing ceremonies, the law-giver with a bold and magnanimous sweep frees him from all possible injunctions and debarring prohibitions of a religious character. The verse also incidentally brings the importance of the *saṁskāras* to the fore which make the twice-born, in consequence of them, what they are and what the Śūdras cannot be. The basic distinction is created by the performance and non-performance of the *saṁskāras*. These endow the twice-born with a right to live and prosper, his social dazzle, and economic opulance, his legal remedies and power, and the absence of these same render the Śūdra a more human entity with his sheer right to exist and with the unnatural gratification of serving the *saṁskṛta* (who have undergone the *saṁskāra* ceremonies) Dvijas and considering through this service the entire purpose of his existence realized. A precarious existence indeed promising by proxied assertion a hypothetical bliss (*kṛtakṛtyata*) ![2]

It is therefore since he is not permitted the right and privilege of the *saṁskāras*, he cannot perform the morning and

[1] Ibid., X. 126. [2] Ibid., 122.

evening *sandhyā*,[1] which act in case of a Brahman would ostracise him like a Śūdra from the sphere of entire ritualism of the twice-born (*Śūdravadbahiṣkāryaḥ sarvasmādvijakarmaṇaḥ*). The implication attending the *saṁskāras* is so deep that it almost amounts to : no *saṁskāras* no sin, no right in Dharma no prohibition injunctions. But this hardly frees the Śūdra from the endless penalization and discrimination he is subject to in law and social justice. Of course, however, since he has no privilege in worship he has no charge to the penalties attending defaults in religion.

And since he could not enjoy the right to be initiated he could not study the Veda or anything for that matter for otherwise extremely grave consequences would follow (exampled later in due context). The negation of this right would further deny him all avocation of a noble character and reduce him to a state which could never in normalcy be the aspiration of a twice-born which again would be a patent byword to condemn the high-caste Hindu with (*Śūdratvam*, *vṛṣalatvam*).

With great vehemence, therefore, does Manu enjoin : 'No counsel must be given to the Śūdra (*na śūdrasya matim dadyāt*) , nor the left-over food (in *śrāddha*, the Brahman and the relations of the deceased alone being the recepients of the funerary food) either; no Dharma must be preached to him (*na cāsyopadiśeddharmam*) nor must he be initiated into ritualistic observances (*na cāsyavratamādiśet*).[2] Those that have the daring to defy this injunction by instructing the Śūdra in Dharma and in the observance of a religious vow (*vrata*) are visited with the prospect of entering on death the intensely dark hell called *Asaṁvṛta*. Of course the Śūdra himself has to share this punishment with him (*tenaiva saha*).[3] The feeling against the ceremony of initiation for and the wearing of the sacred thread by a Śūdra was so overpowering that the celebrated code losing all equitable proportion prescribes the penalty of death for him. The idea is, which, however, is true, that the Śūdra in that case is an imposter (*dvijaliṅga*)[4] and that he must be visited with an examplary punishment, forfeiting his very life. It seems that the profits gained by the Brahman

[1] Ibid., II. 103.
[2] Ibid., IV. 80.
[3] Ibid., IV. 81.
[4] Ibid., IX. 224.

in consequence of his being one was such that it almost corrupted the Śūdra, in a few cases, when aroused by the cupidity of gain and more perhaps to escape the endless pinpricks in life he would adopt the ways and wear the signs of the Brahman. This idea has again been reflected in the phrase (*anāryānārya-liṅginaḥ*).[1]

Manu in the instance of *saṁskāras* makes no distinction between a son begotten by a Brahman on an *anāryā* (Śūdrā) and one begotten on an *āryā* (Brahman) by an *anārya* (*Ś*ūdra) for in the matter of the *saṁskāras* they are the same. The fact of both of them (*tau ubhou*) being 'uninitiable' (*asaṁskāryau*) he considers established order (*vyavasthitaḥ dharmaḥ*).[2] But this instance is indeed in respect of a mixed caste and may be discussed in its own place.

The denial of the right of *saṁskāras* thus cut the ground under the feet of the Śūdra and he became almost an out-caste although living within the range of the four castes. He was as a result ousted from all religious ceremonies and social rights, in fact reduced to a mere living creature and there is no wonder that he should have been classed with mongooses and cats[3] and that even the penalties (*prāyaścitta*) prescribed for killing a Śūdra should have been one similar to the *prāyaścitta* for killing the lower beings.[4]

Manu is emphatic in his view regarding the impurity attaching to the food prepared or touched by a Śūdra. Earlier authorities were perhaps less severe for at least Āpastamba permits offering to be cooked at the Viśvedeva ceremoney by a Śūdra under the superintendence of the twice-born. He lays down : "Śūdras may cook food for the master of the higher castes under the supervision of the Āryas".[5] Gautama's instruction is different. He holds, "If the means for sustaining life cannot be procured otherwise (they may be accepted) from a Śūdra".[6] He adds that "If during his (Brahman's) meal a Śūdra touches him then he shall leave off eating".[7]

[1] Ibid., 260. [2] Ibid., X. 68.

[3] Ibid., XII. 43. cf. XI. 131.

[4] मार्जारनकुलौ हत्वा चापं मण्डूकमेव च ।
श्वगोघोलूककाकांश्च शूद्रहताव्रतं चरेत् ॥ ibid., XI. 131.

[5] Praśna, II. [6] *Gautama*., XVII.

[7] *S.B.E.*, Vol. II. p. 61.

He becomes still more fanatical in this regard when he says, "What has been brought (be it touched or not) by an impure Śūdra must not be eaten".[1] Gautama also enjoins a Snātaka (initiated one) not to sip water offered by a Śūdra.[2]

Manu seems to steer more or less a middle course between the two although he is nearer Gautama than Āpastamba. He begins by forbiding the taking of food or left-over by a Śūdra[3] (*Śūdrasya ucchiṣṭam*). Then he proceeds to recount the castes and types of men to be avoided while looking for food. Among them are the Śūdras and men of the *locus standi* of the Śūdra. Among them are the Śailūṣas[4] or Naṭas (actors), Tunnavāyas,[5] (workers in needle, perhaps tailors), Karmāras[6] (blacksmiths), Niṣāda[7] (catcher of fish, a mixed caste), Raṅgavataraka,[8] Veṇakartā[9] (worker in bamboo perhaps connected with the making of musical instruments), Śastra-vikrayī[10] (dealer in arms) and Śudras in general.[11] Then there were others whose food has been forbidden but these may have been castes still lower than the Śūdras. They were— the keepers of bounds for the sake of hunting (*śvavatām*),[12] Śauṇḍikas-[13] (wine-brewers), Cailanirṇejakas[14] (washermen), Rañjakas[15] (dyers; may have been simple Śūdras), Kārukas[16] (soup-cooks) and others. Then the law-giver proceeds to give the various ill effects[17] attending on eating food given by these Śūdras. In one place[18] Manu forbids the twice-born to take cooked food (*pakvānna*) from a Śūdra but adds that he could, however, accept uncooked food to serve a single night in distress. Again there are certain exceptions in Manu in this regard. Food is permitted to be taken from an Ardhika[19] (one's ploughman), Kulamitra[20] (Śūdra friend of the family), Gopāla[21] (one's own herdsman), Dāsa[22] (servant) and Nāpita[23] (barbar). These five have been positively called Śūdras (*ete śūdrāsu*). To this list has been added such another Śūdra as takes shelter with his twice-born master.[24]

1 Ibid., P. 60.
2 Ibid., p. 220.
3 *Manu.*, IV. 211; XI. 152. उच्छिष्टमदिरा and water, ibid., 148.
4 ibid., IV. 214.
5 Ibid.
6 II. ibid., 215.
7 Ibid.
8 Ibid.
9 Ibid.
10 Ibid.
11 Ibid.
12 Ibid., 218.
13 Ibid., 216.
14 Ibid.
15 Ibid.
16 Ibid.
17 Ibid., 219.
18 Ibid., 217-222.
19 Ibid., 223.
20 Ibid., 253.
21 Ibid.
22 Ibid.
23 Ibid.
24 Ibid.

In the purificatory rites and the length of time which must elapse before the Śūdra gets pure and becomes fit to be communicated to also bindings differed. After a death in the family the Brahman attained purity after ten days, Kshatriya after twelve days, Vaiśya after fifteen days but the Śūdra after no less than a month.[1] After the period of impurity another purificatory rite had to be performed to get further purified and the law-giver prescribes different articles after touching which people attained purity. That for the Śūdra was a cudgel.[2] The dead bodies of the householders too were to be taken out for cremation from different gates of the village or town according to their castes in life. The corpse of the Śūdra was to be taken out from the southern gate.[3] Likewise Manu is very clear regarding the castes of these carrying the dead body of a Brahman to the cremation ground. He says that in case of a Brahman dying among his own people his body should be touched and carried by men of his own caste and not by Śūdras, for their touch would contaminate the corpse and the resultant impurity would stand in the way of the dead entering heaven.[4] The implication is that the contrary could be permitted only when relations of the deceased and members of other three castes were absent. Of the two ways in which the Brahman gets particular censure one is performing sacrifice with Śūdra's money[5] and the other is the drinking of wine.[6] The latter makes him a veritable Śūdra. Thus almost in every sphere of activities excepting in domestic service Śūdras' contact was avoided. Their contact was permitted only as a matter of necessity and in way of an exception.

Marriage

Marriage is one of the basic causes through which social relations spring up. From the earliest time literature of the Hindus reflects that marriage was a long settled institution and that the marital laws were almost inviolable in theory. It was through marriage that ultimately the inheritance had to be settled and numerous social and religious rites were performed.

Marriage was considered sacred and unavoidable in case

[1] *Manu.*, V. 83.
[2] Ibid. 99.
[3] Ibid., 92.
[4] Ibid., 104.
[5] Ibid., XI. 42.
[6] Ibid., 97.

of a Dvijāti (twice-born and one of the most sacred and important *saṁskāras* of the castes. It was through this that the so-called purity of blood was sought to be maintained; and although in all times and among all communities purity of blood and race has been a myth and a fiction, people have, here in this country more than anywhere, believed in a kind of chastity of marriage conducive to keeping the blood of the progeny pure. Lapses there have been and nowhere else the gruesome results of these lapses have been so patent and multiple as in India. The great number of caste Hindus, the untouchables and the pariah, tabooed as unclean and uncommunicable, is in the last analysis the outcome of such lapses out of the prescribed range. These same lapses many a time became so powerful and pressing that they had to be countenanced by our law-givers and were incorporated as exceptions in social relations. They certainly never governed the ideals but they did register the possibilities of uncovered social ground and maintained in exceptional cases what they condemned in normalcy. But the exceptions became the rule and lapses settled down to a normalcy. This might sound as a paradox for the caste Hindu even to-day lives normally under Manu's injunctions. But if we are to account for the endless divisions and subdivision of the unclean multitudes of humanity arrayed in the closing chapters of the *Manusmṛti* and other Dharmaśāstras it will be evident that the exception more than the prescription has been covetted and lived. While reviewing this aspect of Hinduism which can be shown to have been shaped, in the last analysis, to a great extent by the *Manusmṛti*, we must not forget that Hinduism registers only debit numbers, seldom, perhaps never, credits them. The result is a continuous drain of its adherants from its fold, not by choice but by the impossibility to regain lost social status. So what we see and accept as the bulk of caste Hindus, mainly the twice-born three castes, is only the residue, the hitherto unaffected 'rump'.

Hinduism is at once the most tolerant and intolerant of creeds. It does not proselytize; you cannot become a Hindu as you can become a Muhammedan or a Christian, for you will have to be born a Hindu to become one, and those within the fold are liable to the most rigid restrictions. And so from being the vile, degraded fellow which the caste opinion has made him, the outgoing Śūdra or untouchable, or say, the original caste Hindu in several instances, became viler and more degraded from the kinds of occupation left open to him. The day to day narrowing of the sphere of marriage, the ever growing restrictions on the modes of marriage the unsurmountable ban on intermarriage—all combined to create a bulwark of society where entry was impossible and where even within its fold there were the strictest inviolable little frontiers the transcending of which resulted in a strangely old penalty, for in case of an infringement he was not permitted to stay in that fold, not even where the limits infringed were lesser than from where he sought entry; he would in that case have to completely march out to swell the ranks of the unclean.

The taboos of interdining and intermarriage have closed the castes in general to any possible lover of them and also between themselves *inter se* and this was sought mainly to be effected by means of observance of strict marriage laws. It was therefore provided for a twice-born that he must not marry beyond his caste, or laterly, beyond his subcaste, and must marry beyond the prohibited degree even within the caste. The most normal and the best marriage advocated by Manu is the *sajātīya* caste marriage without the prohibited degree and in effect, the Śūdras must marry among the Śūdras. This was also a much frequent and normal phase in the caste society but when the lapses had to be recognized and sanctioned and a lovely wife (*strīratnam*) even from the lowly castes (*duṣkulādapi*) was permitted to be chosen to give lustre to the house of the chooser, there was no end to this choosing. There could not be any end to it in the very nature of things. Then there were those lapses which in early times had begotten Kakṣivān and Kavaṣa and were even during the age of Manu as powerful as ever in their frequency. The actual case was that despite the injunctions of the Dharma law the Brahman and his following castes and a subsequent final third, the Śūdra fed socially and sexually on the one lesser in the form of hypergamo unions, and back again in that which came to be termed as *pratiloma* unions, and the result was what was not desired and was tabooed withal. But they could not be overlooked and, although many a time not approved, had to be at least registered. Manu uncovers a pattern of society in which although the caste Hindu had his normal household and his legally married wife in accordance with the Mānava principles, he had, besides, a second state, not sanctioned by law. Because the exceptions, taboos, penalties, *prāyaścittas* in Manu are so many we cannot but infer this view of things. The twice-born normally married a caste wife but very often raised a crop of children on his mistresses and keeps and these children had to be accounted for. The women thus tempered might have been lifted, abducted, acquired, bought or married. Any way, the fact remains as will be evident from numerous instances quoted from the original below and after that inter-caste marriages, or at least unions, were not only known but were frequently, perhaps even freely, practised. Here, however, we shall deal only with the Śūdra marriages or refer in passing to instances of the Dvijas counting Śūdra or low caste women in general. The main treatment of the topic which in fact centres round and involves mixed marriages and mixed castes will have to be transferred to a subsequent chapter.

Manu at the very start ordains that a Brahman, and for that matter also the rest two of the Dvijas, must marry a woman of his own caste (*savarṇām*).[1] He then distinguishes between the initial and additional marriages of the twice-born (*dvijātīnām*). The initial imperative marriage has to be without exception in one's own caste for the purpose of *dharmācaraṇa* and those other kinds of marriages which are besides such one are motivated by lust (*kāmataḥ*)[2]. These latter ones are also sanctioned as legal but their merits are only relative and the law-giver recounts later their drawbacks and impropriety. Any way, he says that *asavarṇa* marriages are commendable only in a descending degree. That is, descendingly commendable, or, better, progressively condemnable, are the marriages in order, of Brahman with Kshatriya, Vaiśya and Śūdra women. They are only *kramaśaḥ varāḥ*,[3] and they establish the hypergamous marriages, technically called the *Anuloma*, wherein a man of the upper caste marries a woman of a lower caste.

Under this scheme, Manu enjoins,[4] the Vaiśya may marry both a Vaiśya and a Śūdra woman, the Kshatriya,

[1] *Manu.*, III. 4.
[2] Ibid., 12.
[3] Ibid., III. 12.
[4] Ibid., 13.

a Kshatriya, Vaiśya or a Śūdra woman, and the Brahman a Brahman, a Kshatriya, a Vaiśya or a Śūdra woman. But a Śūdra must not marry anywhere except in his own community for fear evidently of polluting others. His legal wife can be a Śūdra woman alone (*śūdraiva bhāryā śūdrasya*).[1]

Accepting the legality of the *Anuloma* marriages, Manu, however, disapproves of them socially and proceeds to condemn them as impure and sinful. And in this regard he refers to history for he says that never in tradition and history (*vṛttānte itihāsākhyāne*, explains the commentator)[2] has a Brahman or a Kshatriya taken a Śūdrā for his wife, never, indeed, even in times of distress (*āpadyapi hi tiṣṭhataḥ*).[3] This boldness of declaration, however, is questionable for the challenge of history is in fact the other way round, and although the exigency of our discussion does not permit us the opportunity of a digression to establish the contrary, it may, nevertheless, be remarked in passing that to a student of history such instances as the possibilities of which have been discounted by Manu are patent and that they may be counted by dozens and are in fact galore.

However, Manu discredits marriages of Brahmans and other twice-born men with Śūdra women. He asserts that those of the twice-born castes who through lust marry a woman of the low, Śūdra, caste (*hīnajātistriyaṁ*) readily descend to the Śūdra state carrying the family and the children (thus born) along.[4] Then the eminent law-giver proceeds to quote authorities in support of his condemnation of the Dvija-Śūdra marriages and cites Atri, Gautama, Śaunaka and Bhṛgu.[5] According to him, elucidates Kullūka Bhaṭṭa,[6] Atri and Utathyatanaya (Gautama, the son of Utathya) are of opinion that the Brahman falls on mere marrying a Śūdra woman; Śaunaka thinks that the Kshatriya falls on begetting a son on her and likewise does Bhṛgu hold with regard to the Vaiśya. But Manu's main opposition is to the Brahman marrying a Śūdrā whom he condemns beyond remorse. By making her mount his bed, Manu asserts, the Brahman goes to hell and

[1] Ibid. [2] Cnmment on ibid., 14.

[3] Ibid., III. 14. This is giving the lie to the *Arthaśāstra* which mentions mixed marriages—BK. III. Ch. VII. 164.

[4] Ibid., III. 15. [5] Ibid., 16. [6] Vide comment on ibid.

by begetting a son on her he loses his caste (*brahmanyādeva hīyate*).[1] It is not alone that by doing so he is denied the attainment of paradise (*svarga*) but his entire ritualism fails him for his manes (dead ancestors—*pitṛdevāḥ*) refuse to partake of his offerings on sacrificial occasions.[2] Manu adds that the very breath of Śūdrā (*vṛṣalī*) is polluting beyond redemption and so is the begetting of a son on her and that there is no purificatory rite *prāyaścitta* (*niṣkṛtiḥ*), counteracting this deadly contamination.[3]

As regards marriage between the Dvijas and the Śūdras, Baudhāyana permits marriage between a Brahman and a Śūdrā[4] but Gautama disfavours it as he says, 'One whose only wife is a Śūdra female is not to be fed on the occasion of the funerary feast (*śrāddha*)'. Here he is in perfect accord with Manu who endorses[5] this rule of Gautama.

Manu refers to both kinds of marriages, viz. the *Anuloma*[6], descending in order, even as the hair runs downward, and the *Pratiloma*,[7] in the ascending order, as where, contrary to the *Anuloma* method, a male of the lower caste marries a female of the upper one. In fact, as pointed out above, all smṛtikāras start with the presumption (and that is evidenced times beyond number in Manu with positive declaration of the comparative excellence of the ascending *varṇas*) that, firstly, the four *varṇas* are arranged in a descending scale of social status and that secondly, marriage is permissible between a male of a higher *varṇa* and a female of a lower *varṇa* and that one between a *female* of a higher varṇa and a male of a varṇa lower than her own is reprehensible and not permitted. It is significant that these two words, *anuloma* and *pratiloma*, as applied to marriage and progeny, hardly ever occur in the vedic literature.

Pāṇini,[8] the great grammarian, however, knows of them and explains their formation. Gautama,[9] Baudhāyana[10] and Vasiṣṭha[11] all know of them and so do the laterly Yājñavalkya[12] and other smṛtikāras. It is further true that most Dharma-

[1] Ibid., 17. [2] Ibid., 18, also cf. ibid. 250. [3] *Manu.*, III. 19.
[4] XVIII. 8. [5] *Manu.*, III. 155. [6] Ibid., X. 5.
[7] Ibid., II. [8] *Aṣṭādhyāyī*, IV. 4. 28. [9] IV. 14-15.
[10] I. 3, 8. [11] XVIII. 7. [12] I. 95.

śatra writers like Gautama,[1] Vasiṣṭha,[2] Manu,[3] and Yājñavalkya[4] prescribe that a person should by preference marry a girl of his own *varṇa* but allow the marriage of a person with a girl of another *varṇa* lower than his own. *Pratiloma* marriages, however, have generally been condemned by them although not with the same vehemence or to the same extent. Manu prescribed terrible penalty for Śūdra living with Dvijātistrī.[5] Commentators like Kullūka Bhaṭṭa[6] on the *Manusmṛti* assert that as no marriage is legally possible between a woman of a higher *varṇa* and a male of a lower one, all the *pratilomajas* (born of *pratiloma* unions) are born outside lawful wedlock.

But, as we come to the offsprings of these dis-similar castes, we close the subject of the *anuloma* and *pratiloma* marriages for the moment to take up the discussion again in the chapter dealing with the mixed castes. We shall resume here where we left off in the context of Śūdra marriages and the penalties for dissimilar unions.

Among the eight kinds of marriage enumerated by Manu[7] the worst three, namely Āsura, Gāndharva and Paiśāca[8], are those condemned for the Vaiśyas and Śūdras. Of these again the Āsura type has been declared worthy of them.[9] Vaiśyas, as indicated at many places in this dissertation, in quite a few instances suffered the privation of and with Śūdras. Of these types, the Asura is one in which the bridegroom pays wergeld (bridesmoney) to the extent he can to the people of the bride.[10] This was prevalent among the ancient Babylonians and Assyrians who bought their wives mostly through money. Manu while denouncing *śulka*,[11] bridesmoney, refers to Śūdras and asks that when even they do not accept any return in money, how then can the twice-born?[12] This is perhaps only a way to emphasize the ugliness of this money transaction with regard to the sacred act of giving away the daughter in marriage, otherwise it will be difficult to reconcile this statement with the Asura form of marriage which he has particularly recommended for the Śūdra[13] and which involves pay-

1 IV. 1. 2 I. 24. 3 III. 12-13.
4 I. 55 and 57. 5 *Manu.*, VIII, 374.
6 Comment on *Manu.*, X. 11. 7 Ibid., III. 21.
8 Ibid., 23. 9 Ibid., 24. 10 Ibid., 31.
11 Ibid., IX. 97. 12 Ibid., 98. 13 Ibid., III. 24.

ment of money (*śulka*) by the bridegroom to the people of the bride.[1] It is obvious that the times were changing and perhaps the Śūdra also, affecting the manner of his masters, was now refusing money for his daughter.

Economic Status

Such a degraded caste or class could hardly be expected to have a decent economic status. When a man is left free to choose his livlihood he finds innumerable hurdles in the way of a decent start, how much more difficult would it have been for the Śūdra to hunt out his grub when almost every honourable profession, appropriated by the twice-born, had been closed to him. Only the meanial work, manual labour, sweating and slaving (*dāsyam, ātmopajīvitam*) had been left to their lot besides a few despicable vocations,[2] all, however, conducive to the good of his three classes of masters.[3]

That generally they could not have a saving because as domestic servants their wages were little and strictly fixed, mostly in kind, in the form of left-over food, worn out clothes, rotten rice and tattered bed, and salary, if at all (for it is very doubtful if it was paid, Manu, at any rate, does not mention it anywhere), was to have been in accordance with the physical strength, the piece of work done and the need of the family of the servant.[4] And if we somehow accept salary to have been paid partly in cash so as to leave a meagre margin of residue or saving for the servant, we must not forget that this after all was a precarious saving, a contingent balance retained only when not needed by the master. For we read in Manu that the wife, the son and the servant, being absolute property of the Dvija, at once the husband, father and the master, whatever they earned accrued by right to him.[5] Besides, whenever he needed money, of course the exigency has been particluarly mentioned as one of distress[6] (*āpaddharma,*

[1] Ibid., 31. [2] Quoted in the context of the Professions.
[3] *Manu.*, X. 100. [4] Ibid., 124.
[5] भार्या पुत्रश्च दासश्च त्रय एवाधनाः स्मृताः ।
यत्ते समाधिगच्छन्ति यस्य ते तस्य तद्धनम् ॥ Ibid., VIII. 41.
विस्रब्धं ब्राह्मणः शूद्राद्द्रव्योपादानमाचरेत् ।
न हि तस्यास्ति किंचितस्यं भर्तृहार्यधनो हि सः ॥ Ibid., 417.
[6] See comment on Ibid., 417—'आपदि' ।

which could any time be turned to look important to suit the circumstance), the master could releieve his dutiful servant of all the little wealth[1] that the latter might have saved by bits. At least the pretext could always be found when the corrupting might was there.

In fact the law-giver's imperative mandate is that the Śūdra shall have no wealth, no property,[2] and this seems to have been a prejudice in consequence of a cruel sentiment absolutely of a class character that when the Śūdra gets rich he seeks to victimize the Brahman.[3] As a Brahman's son by a Śūdrā he was almost debarred from legal paternal share or, at any rate, his share was, as compared to his caste brother's, very small.[4]

Since in theory Śūdra could have no property, for he has been particularly forbidden (even if he is in a position) to collect and accumulate wealth,[5] he was not to be taxed.[6] But that did not mean that he would go scot-free. Instead, he, as *śilpīs*, craftsmen, would be expected to compensate this lack of taxation by physical labour.[7]

Śūdra could contract debt and pay interest on his borrowing. This interest was out of all proportion and forbidding and definitely much more than what on similar debt other castes were paying. Thus while a Brahman debtor paid interest 2 per cent, Kshatriya 3 per cent, a Vaiśya 4 per cent, a Śūdra was compelled to pay 5 (*paṇas*) per cent.[8] Any way, it is evident that sometimes he *had* money, he could borrow money, pay interest on it, and set it off by putting in manual labour in case he could not return the borrowed amount.

That he had money, and could come to accumulate a little amount, is evident from a verse in Manu[9] who forbids using Śūdra's money for the purposes of *agnihotra*, sacrificial rite. Even penalty or at least evil consequence of such act is prescribed.[10] This view, however, militates against one in which cattle, though not money, could be taken away from the Śūdra for a sacrificial purpose.[11] This act of taking

1 Ibid., 416-417, XI. 13.
2 Ibid., VIII. 416-17; X. 129.
3 Ibid., XI. 29.
4 Ibid., IX. 153.
5 Ibid., X. 129.
6 Ibid., 120.
7 Ibid.,
8 Ibid., VIII. 142.
9 Ibid., XI. 24, 42, 13.
10 Ibid., XI. 43, 24.
11 Ibid., XI. 24.

away cattle has to be done in a different way from that asking or begging from the twice-born, for it was to have been an exaction by force from the Śūdra (*āharet*) and the commentator elucidates that from the house of the Śūdra the cattle had to be taken away by force or stolen (lifted, *cauryeṇa va*) for the Śūdra was never to have any connection with the sacrificial rite, and that since a Brahman has been forbidden to beg alm for sacrifice from a Śūdra the need could be fulfilled not by asking but by forcible appropriation (*balādgrahaṇāt*) and in this way the qualm of conscience could be set at rest[1] (*nirviśaṅkaṁ*). This was indeed a queer logic and an excellent way to defeat the purpose and spirit of law. The fact of Kullūka Bhaṭṭa's even suggesting theft for the purpose of performing god's work is too shamefaced an exposition to need comment. The fact, however, establishes one thing, that some Śūdras at least were affluent enough to own cattle so as to arouse the cupidity of the stealing Ṛtvija and to occasion legislation to justify such an act.

Again since Manu knows of Śūdra kings and forbids the twice-born to reside in a Śūdra kingdom[2] it would not be wrong logic to infer from this reference that at least in such a state the possibilities of a Śūdra's getting rich would not be very remote. Then the allusion to and the sorry conclusion following the accumulation of wealth by the Śūdra (which act, it is asserted, only distresses Brahmanas)[3] smacks of experience and brings out the chances when the forbidden was practised and the Śūdra grew rich. Why, a verse in Manu even says that while the Brahman should get over his calamity through religious observances, the Kshatriya through his prowess, the Vaiśya and the Śūdra should end theirs through giving away wealth (*dhanena*) and charity.[4] Then since the Śūdras were fined for offences more oppressively than the upper castes, and paid interest on debt more than others their basic possession of wealth in whatever proportion may be inferred.

The little accumulation that they came to have and that on occasions titillated the greed of the restrained, may have

[1] ...वैश्यादलाभेसति निर्विशङ्कं शूद्रस्य गृहाद्बलेन चौर्येण वाहरेत् । यस्माच्छूद्रस्य क्वचिदपि यज्ञसंबन्धो नास्ति । 'न यज्ञार्थं धनं शूद्राद्विप्रो भिक्षेत्' इति वक्ष्यमाण प्रतिषेधः शूद्राद्याचनस्य न तु बलाद्ग्रहणादेः ॥
Comment on *Manu.*, XI. 13.

[2] *Manu.*, IV. 61. [3] Ibid., X. 129. [4] Ibid., XI 34.

come from a little trade and lowly professions which were parmitted to them. Besides the basic domestic service (*dāsya*) Śūdras could ply a few trades too which may have been included within the range of the term *vṛṣalavṛtti*[1], the living or the occupation of the Śūdra. We have already elsewhere enumerated the few trades which were permitted to the Śūdras. Their yield may not have been much for the margin of gain does not seem to have been ample. The choice of profession itself was fairly narrow because all profitable concerns were appropriated by the twice-born themselves with the assistance of the state. The legal danger that a Śūdra ran against in choosing to live (to raise livlihood) by high-caste callings (*utkṛṣṭakarmabhiḥ*) was great for he could then be forthwith (*kṣiprameva*) dispossessed by the king of all his accumulations (literally, rendering him poor through forfeiture of property) and be banished[2] from his kingdom.

Thus what under the stress of fines, interests on debts, forfeitures of accumulations by both the king and the master, what under the effect of the extremely narrowed professions, and what under the danger of the forcible acquisition and theft of cattle by the priest, the lord of the castes, for the purposes of sacrifice with which he (Śūdra) had not only no connection but through which he could only earn calumny instead of merit here and hereafter, the Śūdra kept going an impoverished, precarious and intolerable existence. Nobody in normal circumstances and in full possession of his brains would ever aspire to be born a Śūdra for that would mean courting privations, ensuring misery, languishing in want and trafficking in exhausting physical labour without reasonable return, without chances of betterment, without hope for a 'paradise on earth' or merit in heaven.

[1] Ibid., III. 164 [2] Ibid., X. 96.

CHAPTER V

LEGAL STATUS

The legal system of a country is the index of its justice. It reflects the rights of men, their duty to the state, to the society, to one another among the individuals constituting that society, whims and caprices of great individuals, class prejudices, interests and privileges of the legislators and much that is upheld or hated in a given society.

This is the story of legislation from the days of Hammurabi to those of our own. All the systems of law have incorporated tendencies which as individuals and honest citizens we all fight. Drawn up systems are codified interests perpetuated in the locality of time. For a time ideas are fought against as also their holders because they prejudice an interest of a material character, material to some that enjoy it, and its enjoyment corrupts the individual and his coparceners who seek to perpetuate that specific enjoyment in their interest. And thus it is that legislation springs up to maintain the status quo. What is true of the drawn up codes and constitutions is to a great extent true also of laws that have grown in course of centuries and in the exigency of the needs of their makers. But in every country and at all times the same principles of upholding the class interest have dictated the incidents of legislation and codification. In the codes of Hammurabi, Draco, Solon, Cleisthenes, Manu and other Indian Smṛtikāras, the Roman Jus Civil and Jus Jentium reflecting the struggle of the Patricians and Plebeians ultimately incorporated in a single body, right down to the Codé Napoleon the same story, the selfsame central feature has been repeated. India was no exception to this general rule and she discloses through her excellent legal treatises, codes and commentaries on them, as important and essential as the original texts themselves on which they are based, the same reflexes, indeed the selfsame prejudices.

To such a system of law-making as we possess to-day as inheritors of ancient traditions the common laws prove a certain corrective, but without doubt only *a certain* and qualified corrective, beacause these themselves have risen in response to very material and well-defined circumstances favourable to some prejudicial to others. Unfortunately India has not had common law in the manner we understand it as distinct from the local regional law. She has had of course local customs, usages, rights and privileges of the castes, territorial divisions, guilds and of the families[1] incorporated in the most part in the basic codes cut or added in accordance with the exigency of the contemporaneous attending interests by commentators, gloss writers, *bhāṣyakāras*.

From times immemorial instructions of a legal character have been handed down in Indian traditions. Formingthe seed and nucleus of later treatises, they developed in the great systems of Āpastamba, Baudhāyana, Gautama, Yājñavalkya and of myriad others and in that of Manu the greatest of them all. The world has not seen treatises of this character—a code without parliamentary legislation—which are indeed peculiar to India. Peculiar, because they legislated, decreed and mandated openly in the interest of some to the detriment of others. There the finding of the student of the tables of law is not through reflections and inferences but straight through decretal declarations where castes and classes are defined in the shape of their composition. The caste or *varṇas* are good or bad as their natural qualities (*guṇas*) make them. They can be *Sāttvika, Rājasa* or *Tāmasa* by nature and their acts must result in consequence of their immutable qualities which are specifically typical of and vary with the various individual castes. This hypothetical premis gains the status of *siddhānta* (that which was sought to be proved), principle, dictum and ultimately of a dogma; and the rights and penalties are cast out of that precarious mould. Change succeeds to change, disaster follows decay, but the mould is maintained and the forms of society in India from hoary antiquity to the time of mediaeval commentators keep appearing cast out of that mould.

It is not that Hinduism is intolerant; on the contrary it is exceedingly tolerant, indeed more tolerant than any social order that has shaped and breathed under the sun. But it

[1] जातिजानपदान्धर्माञ्छ्रेणीधर्मांश्च धर्मवित् । *Manu.*, VIII. 41.

has been notoriously intolerant within its own campus. Caste has been its criterion in the specification of laws which have been mandatory to all, and the legal system, its pronouncement, has become inequitable and harsh and in the last but simple analysis uncompromisingly cruel. What we are going to discuss now is a legal system which has no parallels in its indictments and invectives based on caste interest.

All decisions are taken on a caste basis; penalties are out of proportion for they cannot reflect a uniformity of character, and the considerations at law take the form of avenging priciples. Wrongs instead of being remedied procreate further wrongs; the prosperous prosper and the poor get impoverished. It will smack of harshness on the part of the present reviewer of Manu's laws in reference to the position of the Śūdras to point out that the system seen in the light of to-day which itself is not very straight is by no means primitive legal crudities like the Code of Hammurabi but contemplated wrongs that have through long courses of time injured humanity. What follows now is an evidence in point.

What grossly stands out in the eye of the reader of the Code of Manu, or of almost all the Dharmaśāstrakāras for that matter, is discrimination in law, distinction of caste and creed (for the Buddhists and other heretical sects are mentioned) in the award of punishments and penalties and difference in the measure and extent of the punishments.

The cases themselves had to be heard in the order of the superiority of castes (*varṇa-krameṇa*,[1] i.e. the Brahman should find preference over the rest of the twice-born and the Śūdra, and so also the Kshatriya and the Vaiśya should in their turn get preference. The Code enjoins on the judge (and care had to be taken to avoid appointing Śūdra as a judge[2]) first to perform the necessary nonsecular formalities like saluting the *Lokapālas*, divine lords of the directions, and thus giving to the act of awarding justice a divine despensation to start looking into the cases.[3] And then after properly keeping in view the purpose (the aim) and failing of state as also the *dharma* and *adharma* (righteousness and unrighteousness), he should proceed to dispose of the work of those assembled in the

[1] *Manu.*, VIII. 24. [2] Ibid., 20; cf. also ibid., 21. [3] Ibid., 23.

order of the *varṇas*.[1] This distinction has been maintained throughout in the measure of punishment, mainly as against the Śūdras, we shall point out the distinction wherever relevant. Here only this much may be added in this regard that while other castes and chiefly the Śūdra are punishable with death in a number of cases, the Brahman, goes scot-free. It is clearly said that there is no sin on earth greater than the execution of the Brahman, therefore the king must not even mentally contemplate (*manasāpi na cintayet*) it.[2] Where others (i.e. if the rest of the castes) receive capital punishment and where ordinarily even the Brahman is liable to that kind of extreme dispensation at law he should be only shamed by shaving his head (*mauṇḍyam*)[3] for that is his punishment according to the authorities (*vidhīyate*). Even if he be the perpetrater of all crimes (literally, stays in all the sins) a Brahman must not be executed, instead, he should be banished from the state with his entire wealth and body untouched[4] (*samagradhanamakṣatam*—absolutely undamaged in riches and in body. Compare the commentator's gloss—*sarvasvayuktamakṣataśarīram rāṣṭrānnirvāsayet*).[5]

The Śūdra has no right in law. And the law-giver does not mince matters or fight shy of the declamation when he declares that the Śūdra commits no sin, deserves no *saṁskāra* (purificatory rite), enjoys no rights (claims) in law, is not handicapped by the prohibitive injunctions of Dharma.[6] This categorical denial to him is significant for it wrests from him all rights of citizenship. The citizen of a state never resents penalties and punishments or grudges duties if he is ensured corresponding amenities and rights. He would instead resent the absence of them. The Śūdra's legal and political entity in this regard is questioned in effect, not only questioned but brushed aside with supreme contempt and callous indifference as if he does not even deserve notice on this point. He has no right to perform religious rites, he will not have therefore to suffer from their attending correctives; he has not the right to the *saṁskāras*, he is not therefore to be bothered with sins;

[1] Ibid., 24. [2] Ibid., 381.

[3] Ibid., VIII. 379; cf. the comment on it.

ब्राह्मणस्य वधदण्डस्थाने शिरोमुण्डनं दण्डः शास्त्रेणोपदिश्यते ।

[4] Ibid., 380. [5] Comment on ibid. [6] Ibid , X. 126.

he has no right in Law or Dharma, he shall not deserve or be handicapped by negative legal or dharmaśāstric injunctions.

Noramlly a distinction in the status of the varṇas affecting law is everywhere made in the Code of Manu but it is nowhere so marked as in the sphere of legal remedies or punishments. The system of punishments is ordinarily severe reflecting the Mauryan times and the stand of the Kauṭilīya *Arthaśāstra.* And in the following paragraphs we propose to give some incidents of discriminatory punishment.

For attacking a Brahman with harsh words while the Kshatriya and Vaiśya got a penalty in fine the Śūdra was awarded capital punishment (*Śūdrastu vadhamarhati*).[1] But when the Brahman offends a Kshatriya, a Vaiśya or a Śūdra in the same way he has to pay a fine respectively of fifty, twenty-five and twelve *paṇas.*[2] Thus while offending a Śudra the Brahman has to pay a small fine, the smallest as compared to the rest, the Śudra for the same offence against the Brahman has to be executed. For abusing a member of the Dvija caste the Śūdra's tongue was mutilated (*jihvayā chedam*).[3] And in this connection an expression explaining this distinctive treatment in law has been added which says that this is because the Śūdra is *jaghanya prabhavaḥ,* lowest, being born of the feet (of the Puruṣa). In case a Śūdra abused a Brahman by using his name and *jāti, varṇa,* caste), the former had to be punished by inserting—in his mouth to the extent of ten *aṅgulas* (fingers, about eight inches)—a red hot iron bar.[4] For preachig to a Brahman proudly on the issues of Dharma a Śūdra was punishable with pouring burning oil down his throat and ears.[5] The following verse elucidates that such an offence on the part of a sajātīya or members of the same caste would not be out of the normal and the ordinary and so the penalty prescribed is for the Śūdra alone for his overbearing conduct. As between Vaiśya and Śūdra in such circumstances the harshness of the cutting away of the tongue is mitigated by the prescription of fines instead.[6] Manū's bold injunction (*anuśāsana*) further ordains that with whatever limb a man of a low caste (*Antyajaḥ* may mean the untouchable) hurts one of the

[1] Ibid., VIII. 267. [2] Ibid., 268. [3] Ibid., 270.
[4] Ibid., 271. [5] Ibid., 272. [6] Ibid., 277.

higher castes even that limb shall be cut off.[1] Here the word Antyaja has been used, and although it has strictly a specific connotation—the commentator explains it for a Śūdra.[2] Gautama has much the same effect and Manu seems to follow him in spirit. Gautama says, "A fine of a hundred *paṇas* should be realized from a Śūdra striving to be equal to a Brahman in a bed or seat, or treating a Brahman on the road as an equal. Similarly a fine of equal value should be realised from a Kshatriya who might have badly treated a Brahman, whereas the fine should be doubled in cases of actual assault. For the offence of rudely treating a Brahman, a Vaiśya should be punished with a fine of two hundred and fifty *paṇas*, (on the other hand) for the offence of rudely handling a Kshatriya, a Brahman should be made to pay a money penalty of fifty *paṇas* while his punishment for rudely behaving with a Vaiśya would amount to a fine of half as much. No Brahman should be punished for mishandling a Śūdra.[3]"

Manu after generalizing on the punishment of a Śūdra regarding the mutilation of his limb offending Dvijas proceeds to specifically elucidate the same. If the Śūdra has committed the offence of assaulting a member of the twice-born castes he shall have his hand cut off or the foot in case that has committed the dreaded offence with it.[4] If a Śūdra dares sit with a Brahman on the same seat he should be branded and banished or punished instead with untellable mutilation.[5] For spitting on a Brahman a Śūdra's lips had to be cut off and for throwing urine and filth on him other extremely painful mutilations would follow.[6] Of a Śūdra holding the hair or touching the beard or neck with feet of a Brahman the two hands shall be cut off irrespective of the thought if the act has caused pain to the Brahman or not (*avicārayan*).[7]

For cirminally assaulting an unprotected Brahman woman Śūdra is awarded capital punishment,[8] it being immaterial whether the woman acquieses in the act or not.[9] Terrible

[1] Ibid., 279. [2] *Antyajaḥ śūdro,* comment on ibid.
[3] Daṭta, *Studies in Ind. So. Po.*, pp. 174-175.
[4] *Manu.*, VIII, 280.
[5] Ibid., 281. cf. *Yājñavalkya*, V. 20 for similar punishment for like offence. [6] *Manu.*, VIII. 282. [7] Ibid., 283, vide comment on same.
[8] Ibid., 359; 366. [9] See comment on ibid., 366.

penalty for a Śūdra is likewise prescribed for approaching a woman of higher castes whether protected or unprotected.[1] The *Arthaśāstra* of Kauṭilya prescribes similar penalty in like offence. It says, 'A Kshatriya committing adultary with an unguarded Brahman woman shall be punished with the highest amercement, a Vaisya doing the same shall be deprived of his entire property and the Śūdra shall be burnt alive wound round in mats."[2] Manu prescribes similar burning of Śūdra, and in this case also of the Kshatriya and Vaiśya, for knowing a protected Brahman woman.[3] Vasiṣṭha follows the same spirit when he prescribes that "If a Sudra knows a Brahman woman (the king) shall cause the Śūdra to be packed up in *virana* grass and thrown into a fire. If a Kshatriya knows a Brahman woman (the king) shall cause the Kshatriya to be tied up with the blades of *śara* grass and get him thrown into fire."[4] The Brahman going with a protected Brahman woman against her will shall pay a fine only of a thousand *paṇas* while for committing the same act with a similar woman with her will only a fine of five hundred.[5] He, however, cann ever be executed for any offence.[6] The members of the upper three castes for knowing a Vrātya woman get away with a mere fine.[7] The Kshatriyas and Vaiśyas for knowing a protected Śūdra woman shall pay a fine of a thousand *paṇas*[8] and a a Brahman that of five hundred for knowing an unprotected Kshatriya, Vaiśya or Śūdra woman, and again a thousand for an untouchable woman[9], for she is a pariah.

The punishment to Śūdra for putting on a sacred thread and other signs of the twice-born is extremely severe, death.[10] The same idea has been reflected in another verse[11] where Anārya (Śūdra) donning Ārya's dress and form has been denounced. The impersonation of an imposter is certainly objectionable but if circumstances created are such that people are constrained to be abnormal matters have then to be treated

[1] Ibid., 375. [2] Translated by Shamasastry, pp. 282-85. (BK. IV. ch. 13).
[3] *Manu.*, VIII. 377. [4] *Vasiṣṭha Saṁhitā*, XIX. Trans.
[5] *Manu.*, VIII. 378. [6] Ibid., 379-81. [7] Ibid., 373.
[8] Ibid., VIII. 384. [9] Ibid., 385.
[10] Ibid., IX. 224. यज्ञोपवीतादिद्विजचिह्नधारिण:—comment on same.
[11] Ibid., 260.

in a different way. Any way, this kind of affectation on the part of the Śūdra has been taken exception to and sought to be remedied by making it punishable with death. It is needless to say that the penalty is beyond all equitable proportions and can easily be dubbed as unreasonable at law, to say the least. And if simple impersonation can be punishable with death, capital punishment[1] for murdering a Brahman is quite in the spirit. Only forfeiture of all possessions of the murderer and the utilization of all painful means and third degree methods before putting such an offender to death may to some appear objectionable although that too may not be out of place in the *Manusmṛti*, a document reproducing in a number of ways the system of punishment of the Imperial Mauryas whose laws are the last word on severity.

The punishment did not end with mere fines, capital punishments and application of painful processes and tortures before execution, but included among others flogging of the culprits. Flogging[2] (*siphā-prahāra*) was indeed quite in favour and although it does not refer strictly relevantly to our context, without doubt this too might have formed an item of those tortures and tortuous appliances which sought to correct or intimidate or even register a revenge against the unfortunate victim of this scriptural law. Some times the world presents the strangest paradoxes in life. Many a time the unkindest cut comes from the most humane against woman, and certainly almost always the cruellest persecutions have been perpetrated by religions. No wonder if the *Manusmṛti* also presented in a good number of places a partisan picture.

At any rate, we have a reference to the flogging of the slave and the servants (*dāsa preṣya*) with a lash of ropes (*rajjvā*) or bamboo sticks (*veṇudalena*).[3] This allusion, however, is not wholly unqualified as it is not exclusively used with reference to the domestic but seeks to meet out the same treatment to the wife, son and direct (obviously younger) brother alike in consequence of mistakes or crimes committed by them. In this case the state does not execute the punishment but permits the master to do it with respect of his slave or the domestic. It is, however, ordained that they must be beaten only on the back and never on the upper part of the body on pain of thief's

[1] Ibid., 248. [2] Ibid., VIII. 369. [3] Ibid., VIII. 299.

punishment.[1] For negligence also the servant (*bhṛtya*) could be punished with fines.[2] Fines of various kinds incidental to numberous crimes, legal and social, were exacted from the Śūdra and we have referred to them wherever they have occurred. Besides receiving corporeal punishment the Śūdra paid a good deal of fine, and where he was not able to pay the fine he was expected to compensate it through executing manual labour.[3] This punishment is also not exclusively for the Śūdra because the Kshatriyas and Vaiśyas also have been particularly left out with the remark that he must pay the fine slowly and must not be made to work. This was in case the recepients of the fine-punishment were poor otherwise the realisation of the fines was an imperative course of law.

Fines are also mentioned regarding damages of broken vessels of leather, wood and clay which were to amount to five times of the value.[4] But silence is maintained regarding which caste was to pay how much. We may infer here perhaps that this fine was uniform with respect to the damager. One thing is clear that indirectly this occasion refers to the professions of the farmer, carpenter and the potter. The first cf these naturally was an untouchable but the rest two were very probably Śūdras. Likewise in the same context the same amount of fine is mentioned regarding damage of flowers, roots and fruits.[5] Here again all those implications mentioned above are present and we can conclude in favour of the existence of the callings of flower and fruit sellers. Garland makers and vegetable and fruit growers were certainly in abundance in the country and the state sought to protect them too and to arrange for compensation from those who advertantly or inadvertantly damaged these crops either in their live state or in the market place. In this case also we are not able to ascertain any kind or measure of discrimination.

Likewise two other kinds of Śūdra workers—we only conjecture from their station in life and vocation that they may have been Śūdras mentioned by Manu in the context of damages and fines—are the Paśupālas[6] (cowherds) and Yantās[7] (drivers of various conveyances, charioteers). It may be inferred that none of these were Śūdras although regarding the latter,

[1] Ibid., 300. [2] Ibid., 243. [3] Ibid , IX. 229.
[4] Ibid., II. 289. [5] Ibid. [6] Ibid., 229-44 [7] Ibid., 290-98.

if they can be identified with the Sūtas, we may have to return in the next chapter while treating of the mixed castes since they have been enumerated among the mixed breeds by Manu. A long reference has been made to their respective callings, their negligence in course of plying their trade, the damages arising out of such negligence and the liability of the master therein as also their respective shares with their masters in consequence of the loss of part of the herds, destruction of the crops through them and payments of fines and damages in respect of them,in the first case, and damage of the conveyance, loss of life through accident and the fines and damages arising out of them, in the second. The details of these, strictly speaking, would be out of our range of discussion for they, more or less, refer to the processes of legal procedure and must not detain us. A third class of workers mentioned is the boatman[1] but that topic apart from mentioning a few rates of ferries is silent regarding legal implications and so does not merit a reference here except that he was yet another worker of a mean character who may be classed along the Śūdra. His mention here has been necessitated from his occurrence in the context of the award of punishments in Manu's Code.

It will not be out of place to mention here in passing that the washerman and the weavers[2] were also fined, the former for weakening the fibres of the clothes and giving them over to those who did not own them or for wearing them themselves, and the latter for not giving back the legitimate return in woven cloth of the yarn supplied to him. The amount of fines hired, however, was insignificant.

Legally interest (*vṛddhi*) on debt contract by Śūdra payable per month (*māsasya*) was five per cent.[3] Not only that it was exorbitant but it was in extreme excess of that paid by any other caste. Here also was the caste discrimination maintained, for as against Śūdras, two per cent per mensem, the Vaiśya had to pay four per cent, the Kshatriya three per cent and the Brahman only two per cent per month.[4] The method of payment of debit money or of fine (*daṇḍa*) for the Śūdra was the same as for a poor Kshatriya or Vaiśya, for unable to pay

[1] Ibid., VIII. 404-404. [2] Ibid. 396.
[3] Ibid., 397. [4] Ibid., 142.

back due to honesty they were all expected to set it off through work (manual labour); only the Brahman was exempted from this kind of personal service and was expected to pay back his debt (*anṛṇyam*) through slow instalments.[1]

Manu is positively against a Śūdra state. He forbids the Brahmans to dwell in a Śūdra kingdom (*na śūdrarājye nivaset*)[2]. He further says that a kingdom which has plenty of Śūdras, atheists and is devoid of Brahmans falls a prey to famine and diseases and soon gets ruined.[3] In such circumstances there can be little political right enjoyed by the Śūdra. Manu cannot countenance Śūdras appointed to state offices and that is why he vehemently opposes appointment of a Śūdra to the office of a judge (*dharmapravaktā*). He says that the Brahman both by birth and actions, at least by birth, alone must be appointed to that office, a Śūdra never (*na tu Śūdraḥ kathañcana*).[4] He warns a king against such an appointment and of the consequences which must follow should such an appointment be made. Where a king's justice is administered by a Śūdra there right under the king's nose dces his state sink like a cow in the marhses (mud, literally).[5] This is the penalty invoked by the law-giver against the king who might meditate to employ a Śūdra to adjudicate on cases of law.

The *Manusmṛti* abundantly proves that the Śūdras' evidence was admissbible in law courts.[6] Care, however, was taken that he should appear as a witness of Śūdras alone (*Śūdraśca santaḥ Śūdrāṇām*) as should Antyas of the Antyas (pariahs), women witnesses of women and a twice-born of his own caste of the twice-born (as far as possible).[7] A slave or servant (*dāsa, bhṛtaka*)[8] could also appear as a witness in exceptional circumstances. As every witness appearing in a court of law had to be administered an oath before examination so also was Śūdra to be administered one. But whereas a Brahman could proceed with his deposition immediately after he is addressed, *brūhi* (speak), a Kshatriya after 'speak the truth', a Vaiśya had to swear by his 'cattle herd, a seed stock and gold reserve' and the Śūdra 'by all the

[1] Ibid., IX. 229. [2] Ibid., IV. 61. [3] Ibid., VIII. 22.
[4] Ibid., 20. [5] Ibid., 21. [6] Ibid., 62.
[7] Ibid., 68. [8] Ibid., VIII. 70.

sins'[1] likewise, says another reference reproducing the same. The Brahman should be sworn by truth, the Kshatriya by conveyances and arms, the Vaiśya by his herds of cattle, stock of seeds and reserve of gold, and the Śūdra by all the sins.[2] Besides, the Śūdra should be made to touch the head of his wife and children, that is he was further to swear by them.[3] But this was not all and the most difficult thing was the way to ascertain whether the Śūdra was telling the truth or a lie. It was to be done through an ordeal the dreaded method of the Mauryan times. This ordeal was to be in the form of walking on burning embers and being drowned in water.[4] He who walks through fire unscathed (unburnt) and returns undrowned by water, is to be considered one whose oath's purity is established.[5] For, as it happened in the instance of the sage Vatsa, due to the practice of truth fire cannot touch even the hair of the man undergoing the order.[6] This instance Manu is quoting from antiquity for Vatsa was a Vedic figure and his story—establishing the truth against his being the son of a Śūdra mother through a fire ordeal—is given in the *Pañcavimśa Brāhmaṇa*.[7] Indeed a most dangerous way of arriving at truth and practicable only so far as the officer administering the ordeal is not involved in it.

In another instance the Śūdra is included among them for saving whose life even untruth, considered greater from the effect of its use, could be spoken.[8] Then in establishing the frontiers of a village the evidence of a lot of people of low origin could be admissible. These were the hunters, bird-catchers, cowherds, those living by net (kaivartas), and by roots, snake-charmers, pickers of fuel, and such other dwellers of the forest.[9] Generally moving about they are likely more than other people to recognize and remember the spots marking the end of a village. After ascertaining the marks from them these have to be re-established.[10] Of these some at least were Śūdras, others may have been even untouchables. Only among the Śūdras (including perhaps the untouchables, for, as cited above, Antyas are permitted to be witnesses in the

[1] Ibid., 88.
[2] Ibid., 113.
[3] Ibid., 114.
[4] Ibid.
[5] Ibid., 115.
[6] Ibid., 116.
[7] Ibid., XIV. 66.
[8] Ibid., VIII. 104.
[9] Ibid., 260.
[10] Ibid., 261.

cases of Antyas. This by implication might also prove that in case of a Dvija's trial perhaps their evidence was not admissible) the karukas (cooks of soup) and kuśīlavas (rope dancers and actors—naṭas or śailūṣas) could not be cited as witnesses.[1] The commentator explains that the inadmissibility of their evidence was mainly due to the restlessness with which they pursued their own professions besides their greed for money.[2] Along with these exceptions, however, Manu recounts some more from among the twice-born about whom no such deviations from truth could be possible (although the commentator is not at a loss to find explanations and does throw in some reason however far from the point). These were the king, the śrotriya, the ascetic and such others.

This, in short, is the data regarding the Śūdras being cited as witnesses in law courts. Within its own limits Manu's visualization of activities in a court of law with all its complicable technicalities is exceptional.

We read in Manu of the various taxes like *bali*, *kara* and *śulka*, but the Śūdra seems to have been exempt from their payment. A verse in the *Manusmṛti* makes it abundantly clear that the Śūdras, cooks of soup—Kārukas—and various craftsmen (*śilpinaḥ*) were not expected to pay any taxes; instead they had to work for the king or aid in the public work with their technical skill for a number of days in the year. But, it may be conjectured, where the Śūdras were following the callings of tradesmen and profits accrued to their commercial undertaking, the state shared their gains.

Now we shall proceed to see if Śūdras had any share in property. We have seen elsewhere that in theory they could not own any property for firstly, they could not gain much through the simple act of serving as a domestic where they got only cast off clothes and left over food. Secondly, they were positively forbidden to accumulate wealth and wherever they did a little bit it lay open to the precarious chances of the masters' appropriation for he was as much a master of his person as of his earning. Thus there could not have been much of a chance for devolution of property but since shares in

[1] Ibid. 65.

[2] स्वकर्मव्यग्रत्वात्प्रायेण धनलोभवत्त्वाच्चासाक्षित्वम् । comment on ibid.

Śūdra's property have been mentioned they obviate the possibilities of a certain amount of accumulation which fact is even independently established. The fact that fines could be levied and exacted from them, and although money could not be begged of them for expenses of a sacrifice, cattle, all the same, could be wrested from them forcibly for that sacred act which incident alludes to the Śūdras' having some property, even perhaps negotiable for debts and interests accruing on them are mentioned. A few lowly professions which seem to have been permitted them might also have yielded a marginal profit and a legal share may have been defined and occasioned on partition. Then there were Śūdra sons of Brahman fathers and there claims at law, howsoever feeble, were recognized.

In simple cases where a Śūdra woman married a Śūdra husband no complications arose. As a matter of fact, it was decreed and desired that a Śūdra should not have any other wife than a Śūdrā. The partition in that case was simple for the legal shares would in the incident of the offsprings of such a natural wedlock be as many as the sons, all taking equal shares.

Manu says that the fact that such a Śūdra may have a hundred sons would not make a difference for each would be taking an equal share.[1] The prejudices appeared only when unnatural marriages, as Manu would put it, between dissimilar castes, created the problem of sharing property with 'mixed' sons. Manu in that case makes a clear distinction between a son born of a *sajātiya* wife and one born of a Śūdra wife, married or unmarried. In one arrangement where a Brahman father has children from women of all castes the Brahman son gets three shares, the son by the Kshatriya wife two shares, that by the Vaiśya wife a share and a half and lastly the son by the Śūdra wife gets just one share.[2] This was under a specific circumstance. According to a different division, of ten shares, the Brahman son takes four shares, son of the Kshatriya mother three, that of the Vaiśya mother two, and that of the Śūdra mother only one.[3] In no case, says Manu, where both *sat* and *asat* sons are living, can the son of the Śūdra mother legitimately be given more than the tenth share.[4]

[1] Ibid., IX. 157. [2] Ibid., 151.
[3] Ibid., 153 [4] Ibid., 154.

The simple and categorical principle which the law-giver enunciates in this regard is the following. The son begotten on a Śūdra mother by a Brahman, Kshatriya or Vaiśya father has no share in the father's property and cannot claim a share therein in his own right. Whatever his father gives him becomes his share.[1] Since this statement negates the previous arrangements under the scheme of property division, Kullūka Bhaṭṭa suggests that this last injunction is perhaps with regard to the children of an unmarried Śūdra[2] mother who is a mere keep and mistress to her twice-born man. Another reference perhaps to the children of the married Śūdra mother is where Manu says, "Where a Brahman begets a son on a Śūdra woman out of sheer lust the offspring is as bad as dead (*śava*) in consequence of which he is termed a *pāraśava*[3]." Does it reflect that like a dead son he cannot claim a share in his father's property? A son begotten by a Śūdra on a slave girl (*dāsī*, domestic maid) or on a female relation of a slave, such one gets an equal share with the natural sons of the father.[4] The above thus explains the Śūdra's hold on his father's property should he be the father of a similar or dissimilar caste.

Besides the various legal penalties pronounced by the state there were some social ones equally binding on a perpetrator of crimes. For these numerous crimes corresponding prurificatory rites are prescribed the performance of which was obligatory. But among these *prāyaścittas* too there is ample discrimination among the *ācāras* suggested for the respective castes. The Śūdra here too finds little favour. His murder is counted among the *upapātakas* against the *mahāpātaka* of murdering a Brahman. While for murdering a Brahman a penance for twelve years is ordained, that for killing a Śūdra only nine[5] or even six months.[6]

What is interesting in this regard is that in the point of *prāyaścitta* with regard to the murder of a Śūdra the same purificatory rites are prescribed as for killing a cat, a mongoose, a frog, a dog, an owl, a raven, and like aminals,[7] indeed not an enviable proximity.

[1] Ibid., XI, 155.

[2] अथवा अनूढशूद्रापुत्रविषयोऽयं दशमभागनिषेधः । comment on ibid.

[3] Ibid., 178. [4] Ibid., 179. [5] Ibid., XI. 126.

[6] Ibid., 130. [7] Ibid., XI. 131.

About the Śūdra, besides the Vaiśya, an important injunction is laid down : that he should be compelled to do his duty by the king as the absence of the same would invonvenience the world (of the upper two castes).[1] If the king was dutiful to the injunctions of Manu, woe betide the base-born and the lowly. For he would in that case bring his rich heritage of the system of punishments to bear on his administration. We have already described the various methods and measures of punishments, but here we may add a line with respect to their classification.

Three main divisions of punishments marking the measures for restraining crimes and criminals are mentioned. They were: *nirodha* (detention in jail—*kārāgārapraveśanena*—commentator), *bandgha* (restraining by fetters—*nigaḍādibandhanena*—com.), and *vividha c vashas* (the various kinds of mutilation of limbs and tortuous executions—*karacaraṇacchedanādinānāprakārahiṁsanena*—*Com.*).[2] To these may be added the fines of various amounts, ordeals of various descriptions and flagging in numerous ways. We have already referred to some of these in due context. Manu even advocates a system in the method of their application. He suggests the punishment first in the form of words of counsel, then of approbation, thereafter of fines and last of all a sentence of death.[3] These were the methods with which Manu's state was sought to be held and prospered.

[1] Ibid., VIII. 418.
[2] Ibid., 310. Vide also the comment.
[3] Ibid., 129.

CHAPTER VI

MIXED CASTES AND THE UNTOUCHABLES

Manu's division of the Indian humanity is not very clear. He divides it into three main divisions, i.e. 1. the Vaidikas who may roughly have included the entire lot of Hindus and those that belonged to the Aryan fold and stock without belonging to the Hindu or the Vedic religion; 2. the heterogenous sects including the Buddhists and the atheists; and 3. the Dasyus who in our discussion may also include other distinct ethnic units like the Yavana, Śaka, Khasa and the like considered loosely by Manu as fallen Kshatriyas. The Vaidikas he further divides into four sections. 1. The four *varṇas* or castes; 2. those beyond the four *varṇas*; 3. the Vrātyas; and 4. the fallen or outcastes.

That a man be reckoned among the four castes or not depended on his parents' caste. If he was born of parents of similar castes he was certainly one of the four castes (*cātur-varyṇa*), if he was born of parents of dissimilar castes, that is, was of a mixed parentage, then under Manu's classification he was hybrid, a *varṇasaṁkara*, and belonged to outside of the *cāturvarṇya*. Those who were out of the range of the four castes have been further divided by Manu into two classes—Anulomajas and Pratilomajas. Both of these belonged, according to Manu's code, to mixed parentage rising out of the four castes. The Anulomajas were those who were born of a parentage in which the father was of a higher caste and the mother of a lower caste, for example, when a Brahman begot a son on a Kshatriya, Vaiśya or Śūdra mother, a Kshatriya on a Vaiśya or Śūdra mother, a Vaiśya on a Śūdra mother. The Pratilomajas, on the contrary, were such as were born of a parentage in which the mother belonged to a higher caste and father to a lower one, as for instance, when a Śūdra mother bore as son to a Vaiśya, Kshatriya or Brahman, or a Vaiśya mother to a Kshatriya or Brahman or a Kshatriya mother to a Brahman father. There was then a third class formed by those springing up as a result of the mixed castes, the *antarprabhavas*[1] or Antaras—under Gautama's computation Ekāntaras and Dva-antaras (Dva-anantaras also)—getting lower and lower in rank and social status as the children of the mixed castes go onp ropagating their race. Springing out of the four castes the Anulomajas and Pratilomajas should have been similar in social implications but Manu makes a distinction between them also. He calls the Anulomajas *Varṇabāhyas* or mere *Bāhyas* and the Pratilomajas *Hīnas*, the lowly or the base-born. The Hīnas are lower in social status than the Bāhyas. The Hīnas, however, were themselves not strictly the Pratilomajas for they have sometimes included even the Śūdrās as the Bāhyas themselves were not wholly the Anulomajas for they have sometimes made to include the fallen members of the four castes, the outcastes. The terms therefore are vague and generally specific and universally uniform types.

A discussion regarding the mixed castes is bound to bring in the idea of untouchability and consequently a discussion regarding the much maligned untouchables. These two divisions of the mixed and the untouchables again are vague and overlapping for some mixed of at least the Pratilomaja type have become untouchables and some untouchables seem to represent stocks independent of the mixed kind. It is difficult always to distinguish some of the two types, some of the professions of these also being identical or at least keeping changing. A general discussion regarding these preliminaries therefore becomes imperative. The textual references will follow in due context.

It is Manu[2] and Viśṇu[3] who for the first time dilate upon the avocations of the mixed castes. Manu refers to six anuloma, six pratiloma and twenty doubly mixed castes and states the avocations of about twenty-three. Yājñavalkya names only thirteen castes (other than the four varṇas), Uśanas names about forty and gives their peculiar avocations. All the Smṛtis taken together hardly mention more than one hundred castes. Now these bring us to another allied topic

[1] *Manu*, I, 2. The chief divisions, however, in *Manu*. are the *varṇas* (the four castes) and the Antarprabhavas (the mixed castes). Others were their *vikāras*.

[2] Ch. X. [3] Ch. XVI.

strictly connected with this discussion about Manu's mixed castes or the untouchables, the topic of the contemporary untouchables.

India to-day has numerous communitites of the untouchables. These are hereditary untouchable communities. The list of such communities is vast and unmanageable as a classified social piece. Fortunately such a list was prepared and published by the Government of India in 1935 and is attached to the Orders-in-Council issued under he Government of India Act 1935. To this Orders-in-Council) there is appended a schedule divided into nine parts. Each part refers to one province and enumerates the castes, races or tribes or parts or groups within steps which are deemed to be untouchables in that province either in the whole of that province or in part thereof. The list may be taken for both exhaustive and authentic.

The list is terrifying and is directly connected with Manu and other Sm·tikāras, having arisen from the base found in them. The list includes 429 communities. Reduced to numbers it means that to-day there exist in India fifty to sixty million people whose mere touch causes pollution to the high caste Hindus. Surely the phenomenon of untouchability among primitive and ancient societies falls into insignificance before this phenomenon of hereditary untouchability for so many millions of people which we find in India to-day. This type of untouchability stands as a class by itself without a parallel in the history of the world. We must not forget that there are some striking features of the Hindus system of untouchability affecting the 429 untouchable communities which are peculiar to India and are absent in the custom of untouchability as observed by non-Hindu communities, primitive or ancient.

Hindus who by some chance come to touch them become polluted thereby and can regain their purity only by observing purificatory rites. But there is nothing which can make the untouchables pure. They are born impue and they bear children who are born with the stigma of untouchability affixed to them. It is a case of permanent hereditary stain which nothing can obliterate. Hindu society insists on segregation of the untouchables. Hindus will not live in the quarters of the untouchables and will not allow them to live inside or adjacent to their own. Every Hindu village has a ghetto. Hindus live in the village, or for that matter in the town, and the untouchables in the ghetto. Nothing like this kind of segregation is known anywhere in the world at any time. The śāstras, of which the *Manusmṛti* is chief, condemn the Antyas or Antyajas to an abode outside the village which gives them their class or caste character of being the people's end and lving on the outskirts of civilized habitat. Manu[1] himself provides them an outrageous dwelling bordering on a Harlem attached to the Indian New York villages. Dr. Ambedkar is correct when he says, "There must have been in primitive Hindu society settled tribes and Broken Men. The settled tribes founded the village and formed the village community and the Broken Men lived in separate quarters outside the village for the reason that they belonged to a different tribe and, therefore, to different blood. To put it definitely the untouchables were only Broken Men. It is because they were Broken Men that they lived outside the village."[2]

Much of this view can be accepted but it is impossible to warrant by evidence that 'the untouchables were *only* Broken Men. They, however, may have formed with others the segregated community of the untouchables living outside the village. Here we have to discuss as to who were the Antas, Antyajas, Antyavāsins, Aspṛśyas that have come down to us from the hoary antiquity and have found mention in the smṛtis, quite a number of times in the *Manusmṛti*, and as to whether they can rightly be termed untouchables.

Almost all the words quoted above except *aspṛśya* are derived from *anta*, the end. Antya has been sought to be explained by the Hindu orthodoz scholars as meaning one who is born last and as the untouchable according to the Hindu notion of divine creation is supposed to have been born last, the word Antya means an untouchable. Dr. Ambedkar thinks the interpretation absurd, as, he argues, it is not the untouchable who is born last but the Śūdra and that the

[1] X. 51-56.
[2] *The Untouchables*, p. 31.

untouchable is out of the range of that divine creation of which the Puruṣasūkta of the *Ṛgveda* speaks. According to him the Śūdra is *savarṇa* while the untouchable is *avarṇa*, i.e. casteless, living at the end of the village, and so called Antyaja.[1] We, in general, support this view of the scholar and while endorsing it suggest that *anta* and not *antya* was the end of the village. Both the edicts of Asoka and the Allahabad Pillar inscription of Samudragupta bring in the word *Antas* meaning the independent peoples residing beyond the empire but in close proximity of it and as neighbours bordering its outskirts. But the question is : How was it that the Antyas or their descendants came to reside outside the village and not within it ? That directly settles the fact of the Antyas and Antyajas being out of the Hindu range and considered hereditary untouchables who could never be purified because by the very nature of things they were unclean and their touch polluted and contaminated the caste Hindus or those who lived in the village.

Antya as a class is mentioned in Manu,[2] who, however, does not enumerate them. Medhātithi in his elucidation comments that Antya means a Mleccha, such as Meda, etc. Buhler translates Antya as a low caste man. But according to Manu[3] the Antyas are the offspring of a Cāṇḍāla father and a Niṣāda mother. In the first place it must be remembered that the word *Cāṇḍāla* indicates one single homogeneous class of people all different from one another. There are altogether five different classes of Cāṇḍālas who are referred to in the śāstras including the Code of Manu. Of course all of these are not found in each of them. These five are, 1. the offspring of a Śūdra father and a Brahman mother;[4] 2. the offspring of an unmarried woman;[5] 3. the offspring of union with a *Sagotra* woman;[6] 4. the offspring of a person who after becoming an ascetic turns back to embrace again the householder's life;[7] and 5. the offspring of a barbar father and a Brahman mother.[8] Despite this classification, and from it it is obvious all

[1] Ibid., pp. 32-33. [2] IV: 79. [3] *Ibid*., V., 39.

[4] According to all Dharmaśāstrās and Smṛtis including the *Manusmṛti*.

[5] *Vedavyāsasmṛti*.

[6] Ibid. [7] According to Yama quoted in *Parāśara Mādhava*.

[8] Anuśāsana Parva of the *Mahābhārata*, 29-17.

the same that he first definitely is a generic specification while the rest have only the *locus standi* of the Cāṇḍāla due to their degraded state unborne by and in contravention of the injunctions of the Śāstras. Manu while naming the offsprings of the mixed castes as a result of their union mentions this first and basic class of the Cāṇḍālas, and others are centainly because of them, i.e., following lapses of a social forbidding and extremely deroga-tory character they come to assume the status of a Cāṇḍāla.

But before we come to a definite conclusion about the origin and initial nature of the formation of the mixed castes, the Anantaras and the Untouchables, let us review in brief their reference in the law books. There is no doubt about the fact that they do describe a class of people whom they dub as *Aspṛśyas.* There is further no doubt about the meaning of the term *aspṛśya* which denotes an untouchable. And now another problem appears. Are the Untouchables of the Dharmaśāstras the same as those of othe present day enumerated, as referred to above in the Orders-in-Council appended to the Government of India Act of 1935 ? This question assumes particular importance when we realize that the Dharmaśāstras use some other words as *antya, antyaja, antyavāsin* and *bāhya* also close to the sense of *aspṛśya*, untouch-able. This may be illustrated by a reference to the various Dharmasūtras and Smṛtis. This brings to the fore another question, whether all these and *aspṛśya* are names or synonyms of the same group of men.

The Dharmaśūtras do not unfortunately contain conclu-sive evidence on the point for their reference is rather unspecific and vague. The word *aspṛśya* occurs once in the Viṣṇu Dharmasūtra[1] and again in a Smṛti, the Kātyāyana-Kārikā[2], but they do not allude to the people implied by the term. Likewise is the case with the word *antya* which has been used twice by Dharmasūtras[3] and four times by Smṛtis.[4] They also are silent about the people the word indicates. The word *bāhya* occurs twice in the Dharmasūtras[5] and about as many

[1] V. 104. [2] 433, 783.

[3] *Vasiṣṭha.*, XVI. 30. *Āpastamba* III. 1.

[4] *Manu.*, IV. 75; VIII. 68; *Yājnavalkya*, I. 148; 197; *Atri* 26; *Likhita* 90.

[5] *Āpastamba*, I. 2, 39, 18; *Viṣṇu*, XVI. 14.

times in the Smṛtis[1] but with the same limitation. *Antyavāsin* and *antyaja* are indeed exceptions for although the people implied by the terms have not been enumerated in the Dharmasūtras they, all the same, find mention in the Smṛtis. The *Madhyamāṅgiras*[2] enumerates the following : Cāṇḍāla, Śvapāka, Kṣanta, Sūta, Vaidehika, Māgadha and Ayogava; while the *Atrismṛti*[3] the Naṭa, Meda, Bhilla, Rajaka, Carmakāra, Buruda and Kaivarta; and the *Vedavyāsasmṛti*[4] the Cāṇḍāla, Śvapāka, Naṭa, Meda, Bhilla, Rajaka, Carmakāra, Virāṭa, Dāsa, Bhaṭṭa, Kolika and Puṣkara. Dr. Ambedkar thinks that here too the confusion continues and rules the atmosphere for, he says, for instance, Cāṇḍāla and Śvapāka both have been enumerated by Madhyamāṅgiras and Vedavyāsa respectively among the Antyavāsins and the Antyajas, but, he adds, when we compare the lists of Madhyamāṅgiras and Atri then these appear to be classified in different groups. He thinks the same with regard to the Antyajas. For example, says the learned scholar, according to Vedavyāsa, Cāṇḍāla and Śvapāka are Antyajas while they are not so according to Atri. Likewise according to Atri, Buruda and Kaivarta are Antyajas while Vedavyāsa does not hold them to be so. Yet again whereas according to Vedavyāsa, Virāṭa, Dāsa, Bhaṭṭa, Kolika and Puṣkara are Antyajas, according to Atri they are not. It is evident here, as elsewhere also in his composition, *The Untouchables*, that Dr. Ambedkar is labouring under the stress of preconceived prejudices and accepts what he has yet to prove. From this classification of the Smṛtis one thing at least if nothing else is abundantly clear that they do refer to the same or almost the same class of people. The fact that some of these have been enumerated among the Antyavāsins in one Smṛti and some among the Antyajas in the other or others hardly disprove the fact that both refer to the same category of people. Antyavāsins mean the same people as the Antyajas. Both

[1] *Manu.*, X. 28, *Nārada.*, I. 115.

[2] Cited in the *Mitākṣarā* on *Yājñavalkya*, III. 280 also *Manu.*, IV. 79. X, 39, *Mahābhārata*, Śānti Parva, 141, 29-32.

[3] Cited above, *Manu.*, IV. 61, VIII. 279, *Yājña.*, XII. 73, *Bṛhadyama*, cited in the *Mitākṣarā* on *Yājña.*, III. 26.

[4] I. 12, 13.

The *Madhyamāṅgiras* mentions the Antyavāsins and the *Atrismṛti* and the *Vedavyāsasmṛti* the Antyajas.

words are formed of the same base *anta*, meaning the end (i.e. the end of the village), and *antya*, one living on the outskirts of the village. Antyavāsin thus simply means people living at the end of the village and the Antyajas those again who are born of the Antyas, residing at the end of the village, practically the same thing. The anology of Antevāsin, a pupil living with his teacher, with Antyavāsin also hardly proves the proposition, for although the pupil resides with his guru during his studies, the fact stands that he is different from and does not belong to the family of his guru and is thus an accepted outsider. Then it must be remembered that there is a certain subtle distinction made in the spelling of the words. One, Antevāsin, indicates a pupil, the other, Antyavāsin, the dweller at the end of the village (one Antyaja and by implication, an Untouchable) but in both the acceptations the central idea of the incumbents being *outsiders* is maintained. Such subtle distinctions in the meaning of words by the change of a letter or *mātrā* is not unknown in Samskirt and the words *devapriya* and *devānām priya* may be cited as a case in point. Of these the first means the beloved of the gods while the latter a goat, the delicious offering of gods' and by implication, a fool. That Asoka used the latter form need not detain us for it was either done due to ignorance and linguistic error, or, more probably, to keep the form of the opening lines of Darius's inscriptions in tact which the Mauryan Emperor copied. Any way, there is absolutely nothing irregular in accepting the identity of the terms Antyavāsin and Antyaja, and of the 'people' implied by them. The plea that some Smṛtis are silent regarding some while others add a few other names must be dismissed as an incident of *argumentum ex-silentio*.

The fact of the dissimilarity between the Antyas, Antyajas, Aspṛśyas, etc. of the Dharmaśāstras and the castes of the Orders-in-Council of the Government of India Act of 1935 can be adjusted by suggesting that in course of time the narrowness of the Hindu social order expanded the number of the Untouchables and of the constantly falling men to which the alien settlers also must have added their strength. Then just as the caste Hindus multiplied in population in course of the centuries that followed these also must have multiplied among themselves. The stress of foreign invasions which at least in the case of Islam sought converts made some and at least polluted some who when they could not go back to their original fold joined or were reduced to the status of these Untouchables. Again, as cited above, the return of the Buddhist and other heretical sect-men to Hinduism as also of the ascetic order to the married state, directly pointed to the selfsame road to ruin called the untouchability. The same citation alludes to a few other methods as to how people became Cāṇḍālas. We must not lastly forget that after all, the Orders-in-Council reflect other peoples also besides the Untouchables. They include the criminal tribes, who may not have always been of the type under review, and also perhaps the alien ethnic units. Then probably a close scrutiny might show that many a time the Antyajas of the Dharmaśāstras have assumed new names under the Order-in-Council's enumeration.

Before we further discuss the Untouchables it will be adviseable to deal here with the offsprings of the mixed castes and of the Anuloma and Pratiloma unions, which indirectly—in the Pratiloma incident mainly and to a great extent—were the cause of untouchability.

Manu gives many names to the mixed castes calling them the Antaraprabhavas, Anantaras, Saṁkīrṇas, Saṁkaras, Varṇa-saṁkaras and the like. Their rise he accounts through *vyabhicāra* (illicit unions among the castes, marriage between sagotras, abandoning of caste duties.[1] The illicit union between an Ārya and Śūdrā or between a Śūdra and Āryā are referred to in the Vedic literature. The former type is known to the *Vājasaneyi Saṁhitā*[2] and the latter to both the *Vājasaneyi*[3] and the *Taittirīya Saṁhitās.*[4]

The Dharmasūtras of Gautama, Baudhāyana and Āpastamba, the oldest (c. 600-300 B.C.) of this class of literature, know of the mixed castes and the first two[5] of these give a long list of them. We have already referred in the last chapter to the stand taken by Manu regarding the Śūdras and the cross-breeds. He

[1] *Manu.*, X. 24. [2] XXXII. 30.
[3] Ibid., XXIII. 31. [4] VII. 4, 196, etc.
[5] *Gautama.*, IV. 14-17, *Baudhāyana.*, I. 8, 7, 12.

says that after all the colour of the mixed caste is similar to that of the Āryas (giving a lie to the colour theory of the origin of the Śūdras and the Untouchables) and, thus colour as a distinctive sign between the Āryas and Anāryas being discredited, the only distinction between them is of the actions they perform and the avocations they follow.[1] Manu recounts their main traits as *anāryatā* (ignobility, want of being Arya), *niṣṭhuratā* (hardheartedness), *krūratā* (cruelty) and *niṣkriyātmakatā* (passivity, apathy to performing duties).[2] They cannot, however, despite their oneness of colour with the Āryas, conceal their true nature which they must acquire either from their father or mother or from both.[3] Even if such a mixed caste man comes from an important (Mukhya, great or rich) family he must evince traits of his *Kula* in a small or big measure.[4] Wherever these (the reference is mostly in respect of the Pratilomaja type of the mixed castes) are born the state sinks and is soon destroyed along with its inhabitants, therefore the king should discourage intercaste unions.[5] For the Bāhyas (here Manu is clearly identifying them with the Untouchables—the Antas and the Antyajas) the only way of salvation (*siddhikaraṇam*) is to lay down their life in the cause of the Brāhmaṇa, cow, the woman and children.[6]

We have already said before that Manu divides the mixed castes into two main divisions—those born of the *anuloma*[7] unions (where the father comes from a higher caste and the mother from a lower one) and those of the *pratiloma*[8] (where the mother comes from a higher caste and the father from a lower one) ones. Manu further says that the "sons begotten by twice-born men on wives of next lower castes (*anantaras*), they declare to be similar (*sadṛśaḥ*) but not sajātīyas (or *savarṇas*) to their father but blamed on account of fault (inherent) in their mother (she being a lower caste woman)".[9] This is elucidated by the law-giver thus, "The son begotten by a Brahman on a Kshatriya, Vaiśya and Śūdra woman, the son begotten by a Kshatriya on a Vaiśya and Śūdra woman, and the son begotten by a Vaiśya on a Śūdra woman, all

[1] *Manu.*, X. 57.
[2] Ibid., 58.
[3] Ibid., 59.
[4] Ibid., 60.
[5] Ibid., 61.
[6] Ibid., 62.
[7] Ibid., 5, 25.
[8] Ibid., 13, 16, 25.
[9] Ibid., X. 6.

these six sons are inferior (*apasadāḥ*) to the savarṇa sons".[1] Manu thus does not give to these mixed caste children the status of the pure born. Their status is thus described by him, "The sons of the twice-born begotten on women of the next lower castes who have been enumerated in due order, they call by the name Anantaras (belonging to the next lower caste) on account of the blemish attaching to thier mothers".[2] Sons of these types retain the privileges of their fathers' caste but they are not their savarṇas. "In all castes (*varṇas*) those children only who are begotten in the direct order on wedded wives, equal (in caste) and married as virgins, are to be considered as belonging to the same caste (as their fathers)".[3] This makes it evident that Manu thinks that a man in order to be of a pure *varṇa* must have parents of the same caste. Thus in accordance with Manu the Anantaras (Anulomajas) get an intermediate status next to their father but superior to their mothers'. They are called Anantaras, belonging to the next lower caste, on account of the blemish in the caste oft heir mother. Kullūka Bhaṭṭa, on the other hand, thinks that instead they become like their mother and receive the rites of the caste of their mother.[4] In that case what would be logical is that the Anantaras would get the privileges of the caste higher than the mothers but their *saṁskāras* would be identical with those of their mothers' people.

It is evident from Manu's code that six kinds of sons begotten by Dvijas on woman of equal and the next lower *varṇas* (*anantaras*) have the duties of a twice-born man; but all else born in consequence of a violation (of the law) are, as regards their duties, equal to the Śūdras.[5] The latter, annotates Kullūka Bhaṭṭa,[6] do not receive the initiation (*Upanayana*) ceremony. This makes it clear that the Anulomajas were considered Dvijas.

Thus the six Anulomajas are entitled to the rites (*saṁskāras* like the *Upanayana*) performed for Dvijas but none of the Pratilomajas for in this regard they are like the Śūdras, that is to say that even when a *pratiloma* caste springs from a Brahman

[1] Ibid., 10. [2] Ibid., 14.
[3] Ibid., 5. [4] Comment on ibid., X. 14.
[5] सजातिजानन्तरजाः षट् सुता द्विजधर्मिणः । ibid., 41.
[6] Comment on ibid.

female and a Kshatriyà or Vaiśya male they cannot have the *upanayana* and other Dvija rites though both parents may have been Dvijas. Commentators like Kullūka Bhaṭṭa rule out all *pratiloma* unions as unlawful and all rites, normally performed by Dvijas, irrelevant with regard to the children thus born.[1] Manu distinguishes, according to the commentator,[2] berween sādhu-Śūdra and asādhu-Śūdra. That born of the union of a Brahman father and Śūdra mother is of the former category and that other born of a Brahman mother and Śūdra father is of the latter.[3] Manu denies the right of *saṁskāras* to both of these types, the former being a Śūdra from his mother's side and the latter for the reason of his pratiloma birth.[4]

Here Manu enters on a discussion of the comparative importance of the seed (*bīja*) and the field (*kṣetra*),[5] in other words of the father and the mother, in the point of the *varṇa* of the offspring and his consequent right to the *saṁskāras*. He establishes that, in fact, the best form is the good seed planted in good field (that is *savarṇa* wedlock) which would confer all the rights of the *saṁskāras*[6] on the issues, but he is inclined to prefer the importance of seed to the field[7] and adds even if an Anārya acts like an Ārya and the latter like the former both are nevertheless dissimilar[8] due to birth. The only exception where a Śūdra can become a Brahman (in *asavarṇa*, irregular, marriages) and a Brahman Śūdra is a continued specialized wedlock. It is a strange type of Brahman-Śūdra marriage to which the law-giver alludes. "Should the family", says Manu, "sprung from a Brahman by a Śūdra woman produce a succession of children by the marriages of its women with Brahmans, the low family shall be raised to the highest in the seventh generation."[9] As the son of a Śūdra may thus attain the rank of a Brahman (in the seventh generation) and as the son of a Brahman may sink to a level with Śūdras, even so must it be with him who spring from Kshatriya, even so with him who is born of a Vaiśya."[10] Thus it follows that in consequence

[1] Comment on *Manu.*, X. II.
[2] Ibid., 66.
[3] Ibid., 66-67.
[4] Ibid., 68.
[5] Ibid., 69-72.
[6] Ibid., 69.
[7] Ibid., 72.
[8] Ibid., 73.
[9] *Manu.*, X. 64-65.
[10] Ibid., 65.

of a woman of mixed or Śūdra descent having a Brahman father marrying a Brahman, the daughter of that union marrying again a Brahman in this genertion, the issue in the seventh becomes a Brahman. A similar process of marriages in the inverse order makes the issue in the seventh generation a perfect Śūdra. And what was true of the Brahman and the Śūdra was equally true of the Kshatriya and the Vaiśya in such circumstances. Thus a change of caste even from a mixed birth was possible, only the process was painstaking.

Kinds of Mixed Castes

The Anulomajas (i.e. born of the father of a higher caste and mother of a lower one), enumerated by Manu, are the following : 1. Apasada born of the Brahman father and Kshatriya mother;[1] 2. Ambaṣṭha born of the Brahman father and Vaiśya mother;[2] 3. Niṣāda, born of the Brahman father and Śūdra mother.[3] He is otherwise called a Pāraśava;[4] 4. born of the Kshatriya father and Vaiśya mother;[5] 5. Ugra born of the Kshatriya father and Śūdra mother;[6] and 6. born of the Vaiśya father and the Śūdra mother.[7] Those named above, Ambaṣṭha, Niṣāda and Ugra, are called Ekāntaras as their enumeration drops out one born of parents of adjacent castes.[8]

The Pratilomajas are as follows: 1. Sūta, born of a Kshatriya father and Brahman mother;[9] 2. Māgadha, born of a Vaiśya father and Kshatriya mother,[10] 3 Vaideha, born of a Vaiśya father and Brahman mother;[11] 4. Ayogava, born of a Śūdra father and Vaiśya mother;[12] 5. Kṣatta, born of a Śūdra father and Kshatriya mother;[13] and 6. Cāṇḍāla, born of a Śūdra father and Brahman mother.[14] Strangely enough Māgadha and Vaideha *pratiloma* castes have corresponding ethnic implications with respectively the inhabitants of ancient Magadha (Patna and Gaya districts) and ancient Videha (north Behar); for long these tracts along with their inhabitants were branded as Anāryas in post-Vedic literature. Here it

[1] Ibid., 10. [2] Ibid., 8. [3] Ibid., X. [4] Ibid.
[5] Ibid., 10. [6] Ibid., 9. [7] Ibid., 10. [8] Ibid., 7, 13.
[9] Ibid., 11. [10] Ibid. [11] Ibid. [12] Ibid., 12.
[13] Ibid. [14] Ibid.

has been particularly mentioned by Manu that the Ekāntaras among the Pratilomajas (Kṣatta and Vaideha) too like those among the Anulomajas are *spṛśya*[1], contactable (i.e., they do not contaminate people by touch). Thus all, except the Cāṇḍālā,[2] whom the sage qualifies with the adjective *adhamo*,[3] are contactable.

Manu then proceeds to give another set of names referring to another group of castes which take us a step further down the line of breed. Āvṛta is one born of a Brahman father and Ugra mother;[4] Ābhīra was born of a Brahman father and Ambaṣṭha mother;[5] again Dhigvaṇa was born of a Brahman father and Ayogava mother.[6] Here in the last instance a pratiloma element was added as a Ayogavī was a daughter born of a Śūdra father and Vaiśya mother.

The Sūta, Māgadha and Vaideha, products of *pratiloma* union, also procreate and thus multiply the hated breed of the low tribes[7] (*apasadāḥ*). Pukkasa is one born of a Niṣāda father and Śūdra mother;[8] likewise Kukkuṭaka is one born of a Śūdra father and Niṣāda mother.[9] In the same manner when a Kṣatta father begets a son on Ugra mother the issue is called Śvapāka;[10] so also Veṇa is the issue of a Vaidehaka father and Ambaṣṭha mother.[11] Perhaps both Śvapāka and Veṇa (modern Bansphor) were *aspṛśyas*—untouchables.

Next Manu gives a list of subcastes born of the union of the twice-born and the Vrātyas whom he explains as pure issues begotten by Dvijāti fathers on women of like castes but fallen due to lack of religious observances.[12] Born of a Vrātya Brahman father and Brahman mother is Bhurjakaṭaka[13] whose other names according to different lands[14] are Avantya, Vatadhana, Puṣpadha and Saikha.[15] From a Vrātya Kshatriya father and like mother are born Jhallaya Malla, Nicchivi, Naṭa, Karaṇa, Khasa and Draviḍa—all names of the same people in different lands. Here the ethnic

[1] See comment on ibid., 13.
[2] Ibid.
[3] Ibid., 12.
[4] Ibid., 15.
[5] Ibid.
[6] Ibid.
[7] Ibid., 17.
[8] Ibid., 18.
[9] Ibid.
[10] Ibid., 19.
[11] Ibid.
[12] Ibid., 20.
[13] Ibid., 21.
[14] See comment on Ibid.
[15] Ibid., 21.

types of the Khasas and Draviḍas like the Ābhīras before, have been enumerated among sub-castes begotten by indigenous castes. The offspring of the union of a Vrātya Vaiśya father with similar mother are differently called Sudhanvā, Ācārya, Karuṣa, Vijanma, Maitra and Sātvata.[1] Vrātyas also have been declared *varṇasaṁkaras* or children of mixed castes by Manu[2] as also all the offsprings of the Pratilomajas and Anulomajas and others marrying intercaste among them.[3] Sūta, Vaidehaka, Cāṇḍāla, Māgadha, Kṣatta and Ayogava beget on women of their own breed children who are similar to father in status but have the privileges of their mother.[4] The Pratilomajas of the Dvijātis are considered better than those procreated by Śūdras.[5] The breeds thus multiplying constantly keep on travelling downwards, i.e. socially from a higher to a lower level.[6] There they assume almost a distinct class called the Bāhyas[7] (outcastes).

The Bāhyas also, in the manner of the Pratilomajas, produced on a woman of the four castes what may be called worse than an outcaste,[8] fifteen in number and a class by themselves, outcastes among outcastes, lowlier than the lowly, ever creating downward the status of those thus born.[10] Ḍasyu (in Vedas out of the Aryan range, here too has a similar implication) begets on an Ayogava woman Sairindhra, a veritable slave, expert in matters of toilet and living by means of the net (catching the deer and other wild animals).[11] Among Dāsyas Manu reckons mostly foreigners or at any rate mostly those out of the Aryan stock thus keeping the Vedic character of the words meaning and generally including besides the so-called 'fallen Kshatriyas'—Pauṇḍraka, Oḍra, Draviḍa, Kamboja, Yavana, Śaka, Pārada, Pahlava, Cina, Kirāta, Darada and Khasa—sll those who are born outside the four castes (*mukhabāhūrupajjānām*) whether they speak a Mleccha (non-Aryan) or Aryan tongue (*Manu.*, X. 44-45). Vaideha likewise begets on the same kind of woman the honey-tongued Maitreya (or Maitreyaka) who strikes by bell at sunrise and awakens the king and his people (with panegyrical songs)

[1] Ibid., 22. [2] Ibid., 23. [3] Ibid., 24.
[4] Ibid., 25. [5] Ibid., 26-27. [6] Ibid., 28.
[7] Ibid., 29. [8] Ibid., 29-31. [9] Ibid., 30.
[10] Ibid., 30-31. [11] Ibid., 32.

for the sake of livelihood.[1] The context makes of the Maitreyas the Vaitālikas of the Sanskrit plays. On a woman of the same class when a Niṣāda begets the slavish Mārgava living by plying boats and known in Āryāvarta by the name of Kaivarta.[2] Karavāra, the worker in leather, is an offspring of the Niṣāda father and Vaidehaka woman; in like manner are the Andhra and Meda (living outside the village) procreated by a Vaidehaka father respecitvely on a Karavāra and Niṣāda mother.[3] On a Vaideha mother by a Cāṇḍāla father is begotten Pāṇḍusopāka, the worker in bamboo and on the same woman by a Niṣāda father Āhiṇḍika.[4] Born of the Pukkasī mother and a Cāṇḍāla father is Śvapāka, the executioner.[5] Antyāvasāyī, worse than the Bāhyas and living in the cremation ground is born of a Cāṇḍāla father and Niṣāda mother.[6] These are incidentally also the Bāhyas, the outcastes, besides being specific castes. It will be seen that the nucleus of this caste expansion is the supposed original four castes and through the process of mating the farther offsprings go the lowlier they become so as ultimately to be dubbed the Bāhyas, literally aliens.

Manu permits the six kinds of Dvijātis—the pure three and their anuloma offsprings of two kinds—to be initiated through the necessary rites.[7]

Occupations

It is not the purpose of this part by our discussion to give an elaborate description of the occupations of the various low castes. We have already dealt with these to some extent, firstly, in connection with the Śūdras, indicating where necessary as to which of the avocations belonged to the mixed castes, and, secondly, along with the enumeration of the names of the various mixed castes in the foregoing paragraphs. Here we expect to give what has been omitted there restating where need be the professions and referring to the habitat and way of living of the low mixed breeds and the pariahs.

[1] Ibid., 33. [2] Ibid., 34. [3] Ibid., 36. [4] Ibid., 37.
[5] Ibid., 38. [6] Ibid., 39. [7] Ibid., X. 41

The occupation of the Sūta is the grooming of the horse and driving the chariot (*aśvasārathyam*),[1] of the Ambaṣṭha the practice of medicine,[2] of the Vaidehaka working in the harem,[3] and of the Māgadhas trade by land (*vaṇikpathaḥ*).[4] Catching of the fish is the vocation of the Niṣādas,[5] wood-carving that of the Ayogavas, killing of wild animals again of the Medas, Āndhras, Cuñcus and the Madgus.[6] Here Manu is introducing two other elements those of the Cuñcus and the Madgus to the caste layer without enumerating them in their context. These, however, as explained by Baudhāyana, were born of a Brahman father and respectively a Vaidehaka and Bandi mother.[7] The Kṣatras (Kṣattas), Vggas and the Pukkasas employ themselves in catching the creatures living in the holes while the Dhigvaṇas work in leather[8] and the Veṇas make pot-bases for musical instruments (*bhemdavādanam*).[9] These callings incidentally bring out the items of trade and crafts. It is significant that while the Śūdra has been enjoined, as far as possible, to keep the profession of domestic service, these lowliest of the lowly are permitted to ply their trade and in multiple vocations. Economically they may sometimes have been better than the Śūdras, the basest of the four varṇas. This was perhaps because either no interference in their pursuits could be successful, they having established as ancient occupations, or because they were conducive to the good of the chief four castes.

All was not well, however, for the habitat located by Manu for the low castes—undoubted untouchables—speaks for itself and for its occupiers. The above mentioned tribes, enjoins Manu, shall dwell beyond the village under the trees, in cremation grounds, near the hills and the woods—there pursuing their respective occupations.[10] He proceeds then to specify the same. The Cāṇḍālas and the Śvapacas must dwell outside the village. Their wealth shall be broken (of base metal or clay) vassels, dogs and donkeys.[11] Their

[1] Ibid., 47 [2] Ibid. [3] Ibid.
[4] Ibid. [5] Ibid., 48 [6] Ibid.
[7] Vide Kullūka Bhaṭṭa's comment on ibid. [8] Ibid., 49.
[9] Ibid. [10] Ibid. [11] Ibid. 50-51.

clothing shall be the garments of the dead; they shall eat from broken dishes, shall wear black iron for ornament and shall keep moving from place to place.[1] One who observes a vow must not seek intercourse with them. They shall transact business amongst themselves; amongst themselves shall be their weddings.[2] Their food shall depend on others who shall give it to them in broken pots; and they shall not move about in the villages and towns at night.[3] By day they may go about their work bearing their distinguishing marks and signs (Fahien, the Chinese pilgrim who visited India in the beginning of the 5th century A.D., describes how the Cāṇḍālas moved in the town emitting sound by striking sticks to warn the caste Hindus that they might not get contaminated with their touch) at king's command; and they shall carry and cremate the corpses (of persons) who have no relatives. This, says Manu, is the established order.[4] They shall execute always by the king's order those sentenced to death in accordance with the law, and they shall take for themselves the clothes, the bed and the ornaments of the condemned.[5] This state of things is simply distressing for any student of socialogy.

We have now dealt with most of the professions. A few more some of which have already found mention in the last chapter are the following:Rajaka, the washerman (*mirṇejaka*),[6] Karuka,[7] soapmaker, whose work was sometimes done by the Śūdra, and Śauṇḍika,[8] wine-brewer. Besides these there were some others who generally wandered in the jungles with their hounds ferrating it through and through (*Śvavat*),[9] the hunters (*vyādha*),[10] fowlers (*śakunika*)[11] and snake-charmers (*vyālagrāha*)[12]. The fish, birds and other animals that were caught were not killed for nothing, for there seems to have been a good demand of meat which kept a number of professions busy and Manu enumerates, besides the types of butchers, a number of animals whose meat should or should

[1] Ibid., 52. [2] Ibid., 53. [3] Ibid., 54. [4] Ibid., 55.
[5] Ibid., 56 [6] IV. 216; VIII. 396.
[7] Ibid., IV. 216; VIII. 65; 162. [8] Ibid. IV.
[9] Ibid. [10] Ibid. VIII. 260. 44 [11] Ibid. 260. [12] Ibid.

not be eaten. The work of the butcher, of selling meat, was done by the Cāṇḍālas.[1]

Untouchability

Before closing this chapter we may refer here to the question of untouchability. It has been already pointed out in the beginning of this dissertation and this chapter that untouchability is an institution peculior to India. Here we may point out that there were two distinct aspects of the thing—pollution or temporary pollution caused by an act of contamination and permanent untouchability. Manu has referred to both.

The first of these refer only to certain circumstances in which when once cast a member of the Varṇas was rendered temporarily impure and could obtain purity and thereby his original normal status after performing purificatory rites like bathing, sprinkling with water, taking of the *pañcagavya*, giving alms to the Brahman and by various other methods of *prāyaścittas* detailed in Manu. But this phase of pollution can attach only temporarily and to a person who normally is pure. A man of the twice-born caste or even a Śūdra can be rendered impure by touching a Cāṇḍāla, a menstrual woman, and outcaste, a woman in childbed, a corpse, or one who has touched a corpse, and the remedy can instantaneously follow a bath.[2] But this is only temporary impurity and it is not always that these pollute a man. The woman after her confinement or her menstrual period can become her old self again, a man performing funerary rites can become pure immediately after the Śrāddha is over, but there are some who can never become pure for they are permanently impure, being impure from birth. They always cause others impure and pollute them with their touch and while these others whom they touch can regain their purity through observance of certain rites, they themselves can never become pure. They are described with men who were impure like them, who were born and died impure like them. They are untouchables. Cāṇḍālas and many others like them were and are untouchable (*aspṛśya*) and it is this kind of untouch-

[1] Ibid., V. 13 [2] Ibid., V. 85.

ability, peculiar to our society, that concerns ourselves for the moment.

The Vedas do not know of any kind of untouchability. The stage, however, is set before we reach the age of the Dharmaśāstras and we have already stated how Baudhāyana and Gautama besides numerous Smṛtikāras contain a long list of these permanently disabled groups called Untouchables. Dr. Ambedkar thinks that there was no untouchability in the age of the Dharmaśāstras and that even Manu is silent about untouchability.[1] This view, however, cannot be endorsed as the Dharmaśāstras refer beyond number to people who can be termed untouchables, who are permanently impure, are segregated to a particular habitat beyond the limits of the village. That some of these remain even to-day in the some frightful disability further lends support to this conclusion.

As for Manu's silence on the point, we again affirm that this conclusion cannot be defended. All that has been said in the foregoing paragraphs and pages will prove beyond doubt the authenticity of our stand. But we can refer here to a few further points in support of this view. The groups alluded to by Manu through terms like Antyas,[2] Antyajas,[3] Cāṇḍālas, Śvapākas, all belong to the state of permanent untouchability. These mostly have been condemned to living outside the civilized habitat, to dwell in the vicinity of cremation grounds, to do extremely hateful work.[4] They could not be touched and at times even their sight polluted the clean and was to be shunned.[5] They were expected to have social contacts and trade relations among men like themselves.[6] To know their women resulted in grave penalties for the pure.[7]

The fact remains, however, to answer as to how and when it arose. Professor Rice suggests that the origin of untouchability is to be found in two circumstances—Race and Occupation. The racial theory has done considerable

[1] *Untouchables*, pp. 144-5.
[2] *Manu.*, IV. 79, VIII. 68.
[3] Ibid., VI. 61; VIII. 279; XI 58. 170
[4] Ibid., X. 50-52; 55.
[5] Ibid., III. 239-241.
[6] Ibid., X. 53.
[7] Ibid., XI. 58; 170 173.

mischief and has to be abandoned for not only the results of anthropometry but also studies in thenelogy have gone counter to the idea. Even Manu describes the untouchables only as distant descendents of the four castes, originally forming the Aryan stock. Racial admixture, however, cannot be ruled out and racial hatred and conquest may have contributed their quota to swell the ranks of the untouchables. Their filthy occupations may have been an important component of their permanent disability as untouchables. Dr. Ambedkar's theory of the Broken Men of other tribes and beef-eating may also be accepted as units of this composition but certainly only partly.

In fact there were may factors that created in a long course of time the untouchables and there were numerous auxiliary feeders that made them what they are to-day. Racial hatred to an extent, conquest, infiltration of alien tribes, the disintegration of Hindu society and its extremely insular social habits, all these and many others besides created the untouchables. But the most important contributor to their sorry lot was the class interest.

CHAPTER VII

CONCLUSION

In the foregoing chapters we have dealt with the Śūdras and other lower castes as described in Manu. We have discussed their social, economic and legal status from the evidence available in Manu supplemented by auxiliary works and relevant references from other texts.

It will be evident that these castes and classes suffered a great deal due to the disabilities created by the social order of which the leadership was concentrated among the Brahmans. These groups had little almost no rights in society and at law.

They generally arose as a result of the clash class interests and the Smṛtis perpetuated their state through inequitable and discriminating legislation. From the *Manusmṛti* it is evident on every step that that great treatise is a Brahman document and it breaths contempt for the lower castes on every page. The birth of the Śūdras and the Untouchables itself is explained as being incidental to sin. They are there indeed to suffer for what they have rendered in previous births.

Such views cannot be entertained to-day and, although of late the social tension has stiffened again the caste barriers are fast breaking as they should. But it will take time: it will take longer time to see the Untouchables absorbed in the society. Legal disabilities of these groups have been liquidated but social prejudices are still there mainly against the Untouchables. Temples are open to them to-day but that alone will not do. They have been newly denominated as the Harijans which indirectly puts them in there old isolated position keeping them segregated for their status has not changed and their professions, considered by the high castes as polluting, have continued to be their exclusive job. The worst phase in the present day reform movement relating to the Uutouchables is the rise of Harijan colonies. They have ℥en invariably built out of town and they seek to confine the ancient hated principle of segregation. The Untouchables should have quarters interspersed with those of the high caste houses in the village and the town. Inter-caste marriages and interdining must extend its range to include the Untouchables. And the most important cause of their degradation their base economic condition must be removed and revolutionised and a vast multitude of humanity be reclaimed. Indian society, created a composite piece through the adhesion of endless ethnic and cultural units, will then assume a unified character and challenge both the inclement excesses of time and calculated inequities of man.

THE END

BIBLIOGRAPHY

The following works have been cited in this book:

Texts

1. Ṛgveda Saṁhitā
2. Yajurveda, Vājasaneyi Saṁhitā
3. Aitareya Brāhmaṇa
4. Pañcaviṁśa Brāhmaṇa
5. Taittirīya Brāhmaṇa
6. Śatapatha Brāhmaṇa
7. Chāndogya Upaniṣad
8. Bṛhadāraṇyka Upaniṣad
9. Āpastamba Dharmaṣūtra
10. Baudhāyana Dharmasūtra
11. Gautama Dharmasūtra
12. Vasiṣṭha Dharmasūtra
13. Mānava Dharmaśāstra
14. Viṣṇu Dharmaśāstra
15. Yājñavalkyasmṛiti
16. Dharmaśāstra Saṁgraha
17. Mitākṣarā
18. Kauṭilīya Arthaśāstra
19. Mahābhārata
20. Periplus of the Erythrean Sea

Modern Books

1. Vedic Index by Macdonell and Keith
2. Social and Religious Life in the Gṛhya Sūtras by V. M. Apte
3. Pre-Buddhist India by Ratilal N. Mehta
4. Sources of law and Society in Ancient India by N. C. Sengupta
5. Hindu Law and Customs by Julius Jolly
6. Social Life in Ancient India by H. C. Chakladar
7. Manu and Yājñavalkya by K. P. Jayaswal
8. Translation of Arthaśāstra by R. Shamsastry
9. The Races of Europe by W. Ripley

10. People of India by H. H. Risley
11. Studies in Indian Social Polity by Bhupendra Nath Datta
12. The Śūdras by B. R. Ambedkar
13. The Untouchables by B. R. Ambedkar

INDEX

A

B

C

D

E

F

G

H

I

J

K

INDEX

A

B

C

D

E

F

G

H

I

J

K